Girls

Who Rocked the World

2

Heroines from Harriet Tubman to Mia Hamm

By Michelle Roehm

Illustrations by Jerry McCann

Gareth Stevens Publishing
A WORLD ALMANAC EDUCATION GROUP COMPANY

For my mom, my aunt Patti, and my gramma Dottie, who always inspired
and encouraged me to rock the world when I was a girl. And for Jerry,
who was wonderful to work with. I love you. — Michelle

For a free color catalog describing Gareth Stevens' list of high-quality books and
multimedia programs, call 1-800-542-2595 (USA) or 1-800-461-9120 (Canada).
Gareth Stevens Publishing's Fax: (414) 332-3567.

Library of Congress Cataloging-in-Publication Data available upon request from publisher.
Fax: (414) 332-3567 for the attention of the Publishing Records Department.

ISBN 0-8368-2673-6

This North American edition first published in 2000 by
Gareth Stevens Publishing
A World Almanac Education Group Company
330 West Olive Street, Suite 100
Milwaukee, WI 53212 USA

This edition © 2000 by Gareth Stevens, Inc. Original edition published in 2000 by
Beyond Words Publishing, Inc., 20827 NW Cornell Road, Suite 500, Hillsboro, OR 97124.
Text © 2000 by Michelle Roehm. Illustrations © 2000 by Jerry McCann.
Additional end matter © 2000 by Gareth Stevens, Inc.

Editors: Barbara Mann, Laura Carlsmith, Laura Biermaier, and Mya Robertson
Cover design: Marci Roth
Interior layout: William H. Brunson Typography Services
Gareth Stevens editors: Dorothy L. Gibbs and Ann Angel
Editorial assistant: Diane Laska-Swanke

Every effort has been made to contact the copyright owners of the photographs in this book.
Any copyright owner who has not been contacted should write to the original publisher,
Beyond Words Publishing, Inc., Hillsboro, OR. The publishers gratefully acknowledge and
thank the following for their generous assistance and permission to use photos:

Sphinx of Hatchepsut: © The Metropolitan Museum of Art, all rights reserved
Elisabeth Vigée-Le Brun: Courtesy of the Musée du Louvre
Clara Schumann: Courtesy of F. Hanfstaengl, Archiv des Robert-Schumann-Hauses, Zwickau
Gabrielle "Coco" Chanel: Courtesy of the Library of Congress
Mary Pickford: Courtesy of the Academy of Motion Picture Arts and Sciences
Marian Anderson: Courtesy of the Van Pelt-Dietrich Library Center
Sonja Henie: Provided from the archives of American Skating World
Oprah Winfrey: © HARPO Productions, Inc., Photographer: Timothy White
Rigoberta Menchu: Courtesy of the Nobel Foundation
Mia Hamm: Courtesy of the United States Youth Soccer Association
Kory Johnson: Courtesy of the Goldman Environmental Prize, Photographer: Paul LaToures
Jennifer Fletcher: Courtesy of Luzader
Alexandra Nichita: Courtesy of Allucra LLC
Charlotte Church: Courtesy of Sony Classical

Printed in the United States of America

1 2 3 4 5 6 7 8 9 04 03 02 01 00

Contents

Hatchepsut

Hatchepsut . . . had
no wish to be remem-
bered merely for
her sex, which she
regarded as an irrele-
vance; she had
demanded—and for a
brief time won—the
right to be ranked as
an equal amongst
the pharaohs.

— Joyce Tyldesley,
Hatchepsut: the
Female Pharaoh

The Egyptians stood shoulder to shoulder, so crowded was the plaza.
The sun beat down as they awaited the unveiling of the new royal
monument. As the trumpets sounded and the slaves pulled a cloth away from
the stone, people in the front rows strained their eyes to get a better look at
the carving. What they saw shocked them and they whispered to those further
back. Within minutes the scandal spread like a wave through the crowd, until
everyone knew the surprising details.

In previous monuments, Hatchepsut was shown standing *behind* her
husband, fulfilling her role as his queen consort; or standing *beside* her
stepson, as his guardian and advisor. In this new carving, Hatchepsut stood
completely alone. Even more shocking, Hatchepsut was boldly dressed as a

man. In fact, she was dressed as the pharaoh! "What could it mean?" wondered the Egyptians. There had never been a woman pharaoh before. And what about her stepson, who was supposed to be pharaoh? The gods would not be pleased. The *maat*, the ideal state of the universe, would be disturbed.

The girl who would one day become pharaoh was born the eldest daughter to the pharaoh King Tuthmosis I. When her infant sister died, she was raised as his only child. Before Hatchepsut's family came into power, Egypt was fragmented and often ruled by foreigners. For generations, her royal family had struggled to unite a divided Egypt. Her father eventually achieved this feat, and his reign was a time of great prosperity. He was a beloved and powerful pharaoh to his people.

In order to keep the royal blood line intact, most royal Egyptians married their siblings. Hatchepsut was no exception. When her father died, young Hatchepsut married her half brother Tuthmosis II. She was most likely twelve at the time, as most Egyptian girls married around that age. Her brother became pharaoh, and Hatchepsut became his queen consort. She soon gave birth to a daughter, Princess Neferure. Carvings of Hatchepsut during this time show her wearing the clothes of a queen and standing *behind* her husband.

> *Most Egyptians had six or seven children (but almost half died in childhood), and baby girls were just as welcome as baby boys. Popular names included "Riches Come," "Welcome to You," "Ruler of Her Father," or even "He's a Big Fellow."*

Many historians argue that Tuthmosis II was a weak and sickly king, and that it was Hatchepsut who secretly ruled. All we know for sure is that Tuthmosis II died when he was still a young man, and Hatchepsut wasted no time increasing her power. Tuthmosis' son from another woman became heir to the throne, as was Egyptian custom. When Hatchepsut was possibly as young as fifteen, she was named as guardian to Tuthmosis III, who was about five years old, too young to be pharaoh. In carvings of this period, Hatchepsut is pictured standing *next* to her stepson, as she was expected to act as co-ruler until Tuthmosis III was old enough to rule alone. But Hatchepsut had plans of her own.

Although Hatchepsut already held the highest position available to women in Egypt, she wanted more, so she named herself Pharaoh—the King!

There was a *big* difference between being queen and being pharaoh. The queen was merely the pharaoh's companion. She was not even called by her own name; instead, she was addressed only in relation to the men in her life—"King's Daughter" or "King's Great Wife." A pharaoh, on the other hand, was the unquestionable ruler and owner of all the land and people in Egypt. At any time a pharaoh could ask his subjects to stop their regular jobs and build a giant pyramid or temple. The pharaoh was also responsible for tax collection, food storage for emergencies, construction of canals and buildings, and maintaining law and order. As head of the army, he not only planned military actions, but personally led his troops into battle.

Most important, Egyptians believed their pharaohs were divine—the messengers of the gods here on earth. A pharaoh could speak directly to the gods for his people, helping guarantee prosperity for Egypt and protecting it from disaster. The ancient Egyptians believed that without their pharaoh, they could not survive.

Hatchepsut realized that a female pharaoh would be shocking and upsetting to her people. Egyptians believed in *maat*, the ideal state of the universe, and a female pharaoh was sure to upset the "order of things." So, to protect her rule, Hatchepsut transformed herself into something her people would feel more comfortable with. In carvings, she appeared front and center, but flat-chested, dressed in male clothing, and with a fake pharaoh's beard. Her people knew she was still a woman, but these images told them that Hatchepsut could and would serve in a man's role. And since every pharaoh needed a queen consort in order to perform many of the ritual duties, Hatchepsut broke another tradition and named her daughter Neferure as queen!

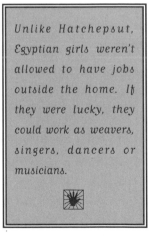

Unlike Hatchepsut, Egyptian girls weren't allowed to have jobs outside the home. If they were lucky, they could work as weavers, singers, dancers or musicians.

It is extraordinary that in Egypt's male-dominated society Hatchepsut's people accepted her as their divine ruler. Even after Tuthmosis III came of age, they kept Hatchepsut as their pharaoh for over twenty years! In a time when the average Egyptian lived just thirty years, Hatchepsut's twenty-year rule was astounding.

The territory she commanded stretched from northeastern Africa all the way across the Arabian peninsula to present-day Syria. Her reign was marked by new and welcome peace, stability and prosperity. She increased foreign exploration, launching several successful trade missions to lands more distant than Egyptians had ever traveled to before. Hatchepsut is probably most famous, however, for her impressive architectural advances. She worked hard to restore temples that had fallen into decay (Even 3,500 years ago, some of Egypt's buildings were already ancient!) and built hundreds of shrines, monuments and statues. Deir el-Bahir, the mortuary temple on the Nile river she had constructed for her eventual death, is considered one of the most beautiful buildings ever created.

When Hatchepsut grew too old to rule, she finally allowed her fully-grown stepson to become pharaoh. Tuthmosis III followed in his stepmother's well-laid footsteps and became a very popular, successful pharaoh himself. Power must have agreed with Hatchepsut; she died when she was well into her fifties, decades later than the average Egyptian. She was buried in the majestic tomb she had prepared for herself years before. Hatchepsut, Egypt's first and only female pharaoh, a woman who broke all the rules, had a fitting end to her unique life. She was buried in the Valley of the Kings.

Hatchepsut was one of the greatest rulers of ancient Egypt. Her reign was more influential and successful than that of Cleopatra, King Tutankhamen, and Queen Nefertiti, and yet little is known about her today. Why? Years after her death, someone tried to blot out all memory of Hatchepsut. Her statues were smashed to pieces; her image was hacked out of carvings; her paintings were burned; her name was erased from pharaoh lists. A landslide even covered her glorious temple at Deir el-Bahir.

> Egyptians loved cats!
> · When a cat died, its owners shaved their eyebrows and tore their clothing to show grief.
> · They often mummified their cats—one Egyptian cemetery contained 300,000 cat mummies!
> · If you killed a cat, you could be sentenced to death by stoning.
> · When royalty hunted, the birds they shot were retrieved by specially trained cats!

Someone wanted it to look as if Hatchepsut never existed. But who? Her jealous stepson? An angry lover? Later Egyptians who wanted to forget their female pharaoh? This is still a great mystery. In spite of these mysterious and sinister attempts to erase her reign, Hatchepsut's legend could not be buried.

In the late 1800s, archaeologists dug her back to life, discovering her temple and tracing her name underneath newer carvings. They pieced together enough about Hatchepsut to know that she was surely the most influential woman Egypt has ever known. Once again, she has claimed her rightful place among Egyptian kings, and the story of Hatchepsut's unconventional life continues to fascinate the archaeologists of today.

How Will You Rock the World?

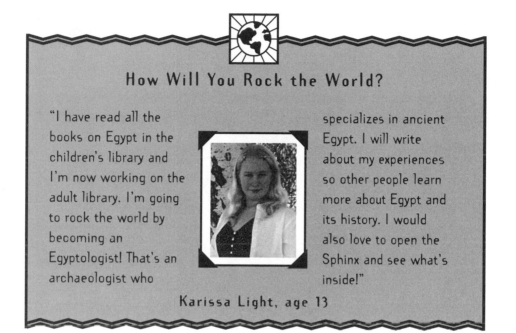

"I have read all the books on Egypt in the children's library and I'm now working on the adult library. I'm going to rock the world by becoming an Egyptologist! That's an archaeologist who specializes in ancient Egypt. I will write about my experiences so other people learn more about Egypt and its history. I would also love to open the Sphinx and see what's inside!"

Karissa Light, age 13

The Trung Sisters

14–43 A.D.   ❧   WARRIOR QUEENS   ❧   VIETNAM

*All the male heroes bowed their heads in submission. Only the two sisters
proudly stood up to avenge the country. — 15th-century Vietnamese poem*

From atop the elephants that would carry them into battle, the Trung
sisters scanned the crowd below them. Tens of thousands of Vietnamese
soldiers looked up at them with pride and fear in their eyes. Fear, because they
knew that, in the 150 years since the Chinese had invaded Vietnam, no one had
risen up against them; the Chinese had more troops, better weapons and more
sophisticated training. But pride, too, because they were fighting for the freedom of their country, and they were led by the greatest heroines the East would
ever know. Trung Trac, the older sister, raised her sword and vowed revenge:

> *Foremost, I will avenge my country,*
> *Second, I will restore the Hung lineage,*
> *Third, I will avenge the death of my husband,*
> *Lastly, I vow that these goals will be accomplished.[1]*

With those words, eighty thousand Vietnamese rushed into battle.

These unlikely warrior sisters, Trung Trac and Trung Nhi, were born in a small town in northern Vietnam in 14 A.D. Both their father, a powerful Vietnamese lord, and their mother hated the Chinese rulers, and weren't afraid to say so. Ever since China had invaded Vietnam in 111 B.C., the Chinese had forced the Vietnamese people to pay outrageous taxes and to give up their culture and traditions. The Trung sisters grew up witnessing the harsh and unfair domination of their people. Even though their father died while the girls were very young, they never forgot his dreams for a free Vietnam.

Their mother, Lady Man Thien, was a strong, unusual woman. In traditional Vietnamese society, women had more rights than women of Asia or Europe. They could inherit property and become political leaders, judges, traders, and warriors. But the Chinese rulers were turning back the clock for women in Vietnam, taking away their freedoms. Lady Thien defied the Chinese when she chose not to remarry, and instead focused all her energy on training her young daughters in the arts of war: military strategy, martial arts, and sword and bow fighting. She knew the battle was coming.

It is most likely that Trung Trac was just a teenager when she fell in love and married Thi Sach, a young district chief. Together with Trung Nhi, they protested Chinese rule and secretly plotted to overthrow the invaders. Trung Trac was described as having "a brave and fearless disposition," and Chinese records claim that Thi Sach followed his wife's decisions, not the other way around. It is thought that the teen sisters were in charge of recruiting Vietnamese lords to fight. When the Chinese governor discovered their plan, he brutally executed Trung Trac's husband, hanging his body from the city's gate as a warning to the rebels.

His plan backfired, however. Instead of being cowed, the Trung sisters were so enraged by the murder and growing Chinese injustices that they decided it was time to revolt. They urged their people to be brave and rise up with them. Eighty thousand men and women volunteered for the revolutionary army; most of them were in their twenties! Trung Trac even refused to wear the

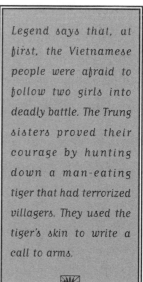

Legend says that, at first, the Vietnamese people were afraid to follow two girls into deadly battle. The Trung sisters proved their courage by hunting down a man-eating tiger that had terrorized villagers. They used the tiger's skin to write a call to arms.

traditional mourning clothes for her husband, so she wouldn't depress the spirits of her fellow warriors.

From the volunteers, the Trung sisters chose thirty-six women, including their elderly mother, to be generals and help them lead the troops. In 40 A.D., after 150 years of Chinese rule, the Trung sisters led their people in the first national rebellion against the invaders. The two sisters were a good balance—Trung Trac was a master planner and Trung Nhi a fearless warrior—and with their untrained army, they miraculously succeeded in freeing sixty-five fortresses the Chinese had captured, driving them out of Vietnam. Stories of Trung Trac and her sister spread quickly, until even the leader of China was shaking in his boots. Historical records state, "A woman proudly led a young nation; even the Han emperor heard of it and was terrified."

When the Trung sisters defeated the Chinese in their first battle, Governor To Dinh, who had had Trung Trac's husband killed, was so terrified that he disguised himself by shaving off all his hair and secretly fled Vietnam.

After this grand success, the Trung sisters created a new nation that stretched from southern Vietnam all the way into southern China. They were elected co-rulers and quickly reversed many of the unfair policies of the Chinese. They worked to create a simpler government that followed traditional Vietnamese values and abolished the hated taxes imposed by the invaders. For the next three years, the Trung sisters ruled their newly independent nation while constantly battling against angry Chinese forces.

Unfortunately, Vietnam's freedom did not last. The Chinese army had more men, weapons and military experience. In 43 A.D., the Trung sisters fought their last battle. Near present-day Hanoi, several thousand Trung soldiers were captured and beheaded by the Chinese, and more than 10,000 were taken prisoner. Rather than surrender and accept defeat, the Trung sisters chose a more honorable escape—suicide. Some stories say they drowned themselves in a river; others claim they actually floated up into the clouds.

For the next 950 years, the legend of the Trung sisters encouraged the Vietnamese in their ongoing struggle against the Chinese; many of the rebellions during those dark years were led by women! Their story was passed by word of mouth from one generation to the next, until the Trung sisters were actually worshiped as goddesses.

In Vietnam today, there are still constant reminders of the Trung sisters. Stories, poems, songs, plays, posters, monuments, and even postage stamps of the sisters continue to inspire the Vietnamese. In the capital, Ho Chi Minh City, a street is named for them, and many sacred temples have been built in their honor, including the famous Hai Ba ("Two Sisters") pagoda in Hanoi. The Vietnamese government proclaimed them national heroes and, every year, on Hai Ba Trung Day in March, the people of Vietnam celebrate the sacrifices and courage of the Trung sisters.

The heroism of the women fighters in the Trung army is legendary. In one story, General Phung Thi Chinh led her soldiers into battle in spite of being pregnant. She delivered her baby on the battlefield, strapped the infant to her back, and kept fighting.

For 150 years, no one in Vietnam had the courage to stand up to the Chinese. Not until the Trung sisters did the Vietnamese people begin to fight for their freedom. The heroic legends of these brave young women inspired the Vietnamese people for centuries, as they struggled to fight off foreign domination. Soldiers carried pictures of them into battle to give them strength. And, thanks to the Trung sisters, Vietnam now has a long history of famous female warriors. Many people believe that if the Trung sisters had not urged their people to rebel against the Chinese, there would be no Vietnam today.

How Will You Rock the World?

"I would start a 'House-Raising Association,' which would allow every person in America to have the roof over their head, paid for, no matter what their race, religion or creed. This would eliminate homelessness and give everybody a feeling of self-worth."

Juliet Eileen Jacovini-Gonnella, age 10

Laura Bassi

1711–1778 ❋ PHYSICIST ❋ ITALY

[Laura] was afraid of no one. [She] fought with clear-sighted determination to win acceptance in the patriarchal world of eighteenth-century science.

— Marta Cavazza, biographer

"**M**ama, Mama, may I please go now?" The embroidery on young Laura's lap was rumpled and frayed. Her mother sighed at Laura's lack of interest. For the hundredth time, she thought that this child should have been born a boy. Reluctantly, she nodded her head. Laura tossed the hated embroidery aside, and was off, running to welcome her teacher, who had just arrived for her daily lessons.

Young Laura Maria Caterina Bassi had a thirst for learning. Born in 1711 in Bologna, Italy at the start of the Age of Enlightenment, she lived in an exciting time, a time of booming curiosity. After centuries of fearing the unknown and being terrorized by the mysteries of life, people were beginning to calm down. For the first time, they began to understand that through observing and questioning the world around them, some of the unknowable could indeed become known. Life was becoming less a terrifying mystery and more an intriguing puzzle to be sorted out.

Unfortunately for Laura, women were not invited to the Age of Enlightenment. Upper-class girls like her were supposed to learn to sew, to manage a home and servants, and to prepare themselves for motherhood. They weren't expected to be interested in or even have the brains to be curious about the natural world. But Laura didn't let this prejudice stop her. Throughout her life, Laura never settled for what other people wanted of her.

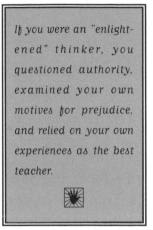

If you were an "enlightened" thinker, you questioned authority, examined your own motives for prejudice, and relied on your own experiences as the best teacher.

Laura's teacher, a professor at the University of Bologna, was a good one. He was also the Bassi family physician, and had agreed, at Laura's father's request, to teach her. He came to the Bassi villa each day. There, in her sunny garden, Laura studied mathematics, philosophy, anatomy, natural history, and languages.

When she was only twenty, her teacher declared she had learned everything he had to teach. It was time for her public examination. He took her to the University to be grilled by the best minds in Bologna. For hours, learned and unbelieving professors, all men, queried Laura about her lessons, and challenged her answers.

Laura not only gave the right answers, she defended them with spirit. Despite her sex, they could not dispute her knowledge. So in a solemn ceremony in the *Palazzo Pubblico* (public palace), she was named a professor of anatomy at the University and a member of the Academy of the Institute for Sciences. In the University of Bologna's 600-year history, no woman had ever been named a professor. Laura was the first.

But, as time went on, it became clear to Laura that, despite her achievements, she was considered "special." Not special in a good way. Special in that she didn't get to participate in the life of the University like the male professors did. She was a gracious young woman, good at meeting the right people and charming them with her wit and knowledge. University leaders thought she would make a great figurehead, a "beauty queen" of science.

They tried to limit her role to hosting parties and welcoming honored guests. She was called the Bologna Minerva, after the ancient Roman goddess of wisdom, invention, and the arts. It was a lovely title, but Laura didn't want titles. She wanted to teach.

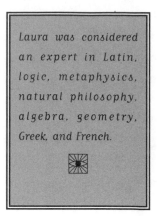

Laura was considered an expert in Latin, logic, metaphysics, natural philosophy, algebra, geometry, Greek, and French.

She played along with the game, earning some powerful friends as she performed her hostess duties. Then she went home and quietly did exactly what she wanted. With the support of her husband, physicist Giuseppe Veratti, Laura set up a private teaching laboratory in her home. There, surrounded by her growing family (She eventually had twelve children!), she continued teaching and researching in experimental physics, ignoring the taunts of male scholars, who claimed that she was neglecting her work to care for her children.

If it bothered Laura, she didn't complain. She kept her head in her studies and in her teaching, and unlike most of her male colleagues, didn't worry about trying to publish her findings and become famous. For her, knowledge was the goal.

In 1745, when she was thirty-four, her years of research and her skills at gracefully handling disbelieving colleagues began to pay off. Laura started to get the recognition she deserved. Finally! She was allowed to teach the "male sciences" of mechanics, hydrometry, and elasticity. The Pope himself, Benedict XIV, nominated her for a post in his Benedictine Academy of Science. But even with the Pope's backing, her colleagues still thwarted her and would not allow her to vote, even though she was a member of the Academy.

Laura was admired for her good character and charity to the poor, and was sought out by famous thinkers, like Voltaire, when they visited Bologna.

Despite the continuing discrimination, from that time on, Laura's authority was questioned less frequently. She had proven herself and shown that women could do more than manage households. Her fame as a teacher spread, and, at sixty-five, two years before her death, Laura was appointed to the prestigious Chair of Experimental Physics at the Institute of Sciences in Bologna.

Laura Bassi was an early hero in the fight for women's equality. Her struggle and triumph over male chauvinism are an inspiration to every girl who has been labeled "different." As Laura showed, being "different" can be a wonderful thing.

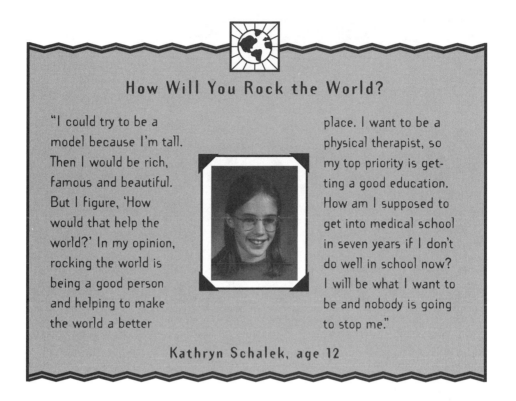

How Will You Rock the World?

"I could try to be a model because I'm tall. Then I would be rich, famous and beautiful. But I figure, 'How would that help the world?' In my opinion, rocking the world is being a good person and helping to make the world a better place. I want to be a physical therapist, so my top priority is getting a good education. How am I supposed to get into medical school in seven years if I don't do well in school now? I will be what I want to be and nobody is going to stop me."

Kathryn Schalek, age 12

Elisabeth Vigée-Le Brun

1755—1842 🔲 *PAINTER* 🔲 *FRANCE*

I know nothing of painting, but I have grown to love it through you.
— King Louis XVI, praising Elisabeth's portrait of his wife, Marie Antoinette.

The theater darkened and Elisabeth had a moment to look around her. She was surrounded by beautiful men and women, dressed in the most sumptuous fabrics, wearing extravagant powdered wigs and sparkling jewels. She was a teenager who had to earn her own living from her paintings! The curtain opened, and she turned her attention to the stage, where a young woman was standing before an easel, paintbrushes and palette in hand. Her subject was a beautiful woman wearing a plain muslin dress and a straw hat.

Wait! Where had she seen this before? To her surprise and delight, Elisabeth realized they were acting out a scene from her own life—her painting the queen, Marie Antoinette! In the portrait, she had tried to show the queen in a more natural way, instead of in her usual elaborate wigs and white face powder, with the result that many people criticized her for painting the queen in her underwear! Not this crowd, thankfully. Elisabeth held back her tears as the entire audience stood up and applauded her. She had never felt so much emotion and pride in her entire life.

Imagine, at fifteen, you are such a talented artist that all the kings and queens and presidents of the world are begging you to paint them! She is still considered one of the most talented and successful portrait painters ever, artist to the richest, most famous Europeans of her time, but Elisabeth Vigée-Le Brun rose from very humble beginnings. She was born in Paris to a middle-class family. Her father was a moderately successful painter and often let his daughter play with his paints and brushes.

From age six to age eleven, Elisabeth lived in a convent, where she first showed her artistic talents. In her memoirs, she wrote:

> *During this time I was always sketching, covering every available surface with my drawings; my exercise books . . . had their margins crammed with tiny drawings of heads and profiles. I traced figures . . . on the dormitory walls in charcoal; and as you may well suppose, I was often punished.*[2]

After she had returned home for a year, Elisabeth's beloved father died from swallowing a fish bone. He left the family very little money to live on, so Elisabeth began charging for her paintings. Although she was virtually self-taught, she had such remarkable talent that, by age fifteen, she supported her entire family on her wages.

Her reputation spread quickly and soon the talented teenager was in constant demand to paint the French aristocracy. Meanwhile, Elisabeth's mother remarried a wealthy jeweler. Elisabeth hated the man, who wore her father's clothes, had a terrible temper, and forced her to turn over all her earnings to him. To escape, she rushed into marriage with art collector A.M. Le Brun, even though her friends warned her, "You would do better to tie a stone around your neck and throw yourself in the river," but she was desperate.

Elisabeth was invited into the French Royal Academy of Painting, one of only three women ever to be included.

Sadly, her friends were right. Her husband earned no money, but forced Elisabeth to give her ample wages to him, which he spent on women, drinking, and gambling. Elisabeth was miserable.

Fortunately, her art gave her great happiness. In 1778, at twenty-three, Elisabeth was such a celebrity that Marie Antoinette insisted she become an official court painter. Elisabeth wrote of this queen:

> I was very much in awe of Her Majesty's imposing air; but she
> spoke to me in such a kindly fashion that her warm sympathy
> soon dissolved any such impression.[3]

The court appointment turned Elisabeth into the "in" portrait painter. She was sought after by royal families and the most influential leaders of her time and earned incredible fees.

For the first time, queens and princesses allowed themselves to be painted in costumes that hid their high social rank. She even set new fashion standards, by encouraging her subjects to stop powdering their hair and go natural. The women were delighted to be seen as beautiful. Elisabeth had a talent to see the inner beauty of even the most unattractive person.

But, as time went on, the decadent royal family became less and less popular. So did Elisabeth. Lies were spread about her: she charged extravagant fees for her paintings, she threw unbelievably lavish parties, she was having an affair with the Minister of Finance. Worst of all, Elisabeth's enemies claimed her portraits weren't really hers, but were painted by a man!

In 1789, when the French Revolution swept through the country, killing Marie Antoinette, much of the royal family, and their friends, Elisabeth was horrified. She knew that she could be next because of her ties to the Queen, so she and her daughter escaped to Italy. They wouldn't see France again for twelve years.

Elisabeth's most famous portrait of Marie Antoinette was so criticized for the high fee paid to the artist that the royal family had to turn the painting so it faced the wall in the Louvre. It remained that way until after the French Revolution, when it was turned back around.

During her exile, Elisabeth traveled all over
Europe—Italy, Austria, Czechoslovakia, Germany,
Switzerland, England, and Russia. She supported
herself and her daughter by painting the royal
families and important figures of each country
they visited, including another infamous queen,
Russia's Catherine the Great.

While traveling, Elisabeth finally broke with
her husband for good. Her letter to him from
Moscow shows what an unusual, independent
spirit she had:

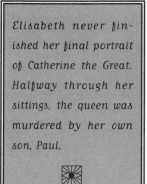

*Elisabeth never fin-
ished her final portrait
of Catherine the Great.
Halfway through her
sittings, the queen was
murdered by her own
son, Paul.*

> *What would I have done without my work? If I had been ill, you
> would have let me starve; since instead of saving money you have
> spent it on women who deceived you, you have gambled and lost,
> Monsieur. I will neither let my fortune fall into the hands of
> strangers, since it has been too hard to earn . . . nor will I take
> advice from anyone.*[4]

At a time when few women supported themselves, Elisabeth chose to be a single mother, earn her own way and travel the world.

In 1802, after 255 artists petitioned for Elisabeth's return, she was allowed
back into France. She continued to paint well into her old age, and in the
1830s, she published her memoirs, which were very popular. In her seventies,
she praised her life's work: "This love [of painting] has never diminished . . .
[I] hope that its power will only cease with my life."

Perhaps her art gave her strength and energy as well—she lived to the ripe
old age of eighty-seven! During her lifetime she painted over 900 paintings,
which hang in such prestigious museums as the Louvre in Paris, the National
Gallery of Art in London, the Metropolitan Museum of Art in New York, and the
Uffizi Gallery in Florence, Italy. She is ranked beside such great masters as
Raphael and Caravaggio, and was an inspiration to female painters and independent women almost two hundred years before the term "feminist" was coined.

My only real happiness has been through painting.
— Elisabeth Vigée-Le Brun

Pop-pank

1790–? ✸ *SURVIVOR* ✸ *UNITED STATES*

We drew near to the camp and just as we approached it, a woman made her way through the crowd toward Sacagawea, and recognizing each other, they embraced with most tender affection.

— Meriwether Lewis, *The Journals of Lewis and Clark*, describing the surprise reunion of Pop-pank and Sacagawea.

P op-pank heard it first—the pounding of horses' hooves. She and her best friend Sacagawea turned to see a scout race past them, shouting, "Attack! Attack!" "They're coming!" yelled Sacagawea, her eyes wide with fear. The girls dropped the berries and roots they were collecting and searched frantically for hiding places. Pop-pank splashed across a stream and dove inside a thick clump of bushes. Just then, the enemy attacked. The war cries and crack of enemy "fire sticks" echoed in her head.

Suddenly, a hand reached into the bushes and tore Pop-pank from her hiding place. She kicked and screamed, but it was no use. Her captor was a grown man, a warrior, and she was a small girl. He yanked her up onto his horse and galloped off. Through her tears of frustration and fear, Pop-pank saw another horse and rider following them, with another prisoner. She wasn't sure whether to be happy or sad when she recognized Sacagawea. As the horses rode swiftly east, and her home and people became more and more distant, Pop-pank vowed that she would escape. Nothing would stop her from returning to her beloved home.

The attack was over in minutes, but those minutes changed the lives of Sacagawea and Pop-pank forever. It would even change the history of the U.S. One of the girls would become world-famous for her heroic deeds, but would suffer estrangement from her people. The other would never be famous, but her strength and courage would bring her lasting happiness with her family and friends. As the two eleven-year-olds were carried off to uncertain futures, neither knew what different roads their lives would take.

Pop-pank was born sometime around 1790 to the Shoshoni (sho-sho-nee) people of what is now called Idaho. The Shoshoni were a peaceful tribe who struggled to survive the harsh winters of their mountain home. In the fall each year, they had to move from the protective peaks into the vast, open prairies of western Montana to hunt buffalo. They needed the meat, skin and bones of the buffalo for food, shelter, clothing and tools. Without buffalo, the Shoshoni could not survive.

But these journeys were extremely dangerous. When white men had first arrived in North America decades before, they brought horses and guns to the tribes. The Shoshoni got horses, but no guns, so they were vulnerable to attack by their enemies. Many of the more warlike tribes of the prairie—the Crow, Blackfoot, and Minnetare (min-ne-tar-e)—knew the Shoshoni would come for buffalo each year. They sent raiding parties to steal the Shoshoni's horses, kill their warriors, and kidnap the women and children.

When Pop-pank and Sacagawea were eleven, their tribe was attacked by the Minnetare, near Three Forks, Montana. When the raid was over and the dust settled, the Shoshoni mourned their losses. Many people had been killed, and fifteen women and children had been kidnapped. Pop-pank, Sacagawea, and the other captives were marched over 1,000 miles (1,609 kilometers), on foot, from western Montana to present-day Mandan, North Dakota (home to the Minnetare).

There is no written record of their march, but from the journals of Lewis and Clark, who traveled the same route a few years later, we can imagine what it must have been like for the prisoners. They hiked in deerskin moccasins across a land covered with prickly pear cactus. The sharp thorns would have easily pierced their shoes, causing them great pain. Escape would have been impossible with the Minnetare watching their every move and the open plains offering few hiding places. Prisoners who tried to escape would have been killed on the spot.

Pop-pank surely knew this, and instead of trying an immediate escape, spent her energy memorizing their route. As they followed the Missouri River, she noted each turn of the river and major landmarks, and scoped out good hiding places for a later escape. The journey would have taken the group over a month to make. Imagine being forced to march over thirty miles (48 km) a day, your feet burning and your heart crying in silent frustration. When they arrived at the Minnetare village, the prisoners were distributed to various families to use as slaves.

Indian slaves, like African slaves on white plantations in the South, lived their lives at their masters' whims. They were beaten regularly and had to work from dawn until dusk. Friends and relatives were split up forever when slaves were traded to other tribes or to white men.

Not long after bringing the Shoshoni prisoners to their village, a few Minnetare warriors lost a card game with Pierre Charbonneau, a French fur trapper. To pay their debt, they offered him eleven-year-old Sacagawea, to take as his "wife." Although Charbonneau already had several other young Indian wives, he accepted their payment. Sacagawea had no choice but to leave for even more distant lands with this white stranger, her new master.

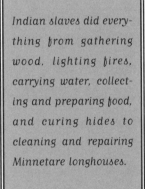

Indian slaves did everything from gathering wood, lighting fires, carrying water, collecting and preparing food, and curing hides to cleaning and repairing Minnetare longhouses.

The loss of her best friend undoubtedly panicked Pop-pank, who realized she, too, could be traded away at any time, making her chances of returning home almost impossible. She had to make her move soon. How she escaped we can only guess, but we do know she was kidnapped in August, so she likely fled that fall. If Pop-pank merely bolted, with no plan or supplies, she would never have made it back to Idaho. To survive the long, difficult journey Pop-pank needed the courage not only to escape her masters, but also to steal what she would need to make it home: warm clothing, something to hunt with, and a supply of food to last until she was far away from the Minnetare village.

Pop-pank must have been terrified when she finally sneaked away—she would have been killed if she was caught. And yet the dangers were only beginning. When Lewis and Clark covered the same ground a few years later with more than a dozen armed men, they barely survived. Pop-pank had to be on constant alert for other Indians who might enslave her again, as well as for wolves, grizzly bears, stampeding buffalo, snowstorms, and even mosquitoes, which carried the deadly malaria. For a lone girl to survive, she had to be not only brave, but also very smart.

It is hard to imagine an eleven-year-old girl walking from North Dakota to Idaho—by herself! And Pop-pank did it with no roads, no signs, no maps, no McDonald's, no tent, no boots, no rain-coat—nothing! She followed the Missouri River, remembering the landmarks she'd seen before. Even in the snow, she had to sleep outdoors, with nothing but a buffalo hide to keep her warm. For at least a month, she had to find or kill anything she ate. Even cooking was a long, difficult ordeal with no matches or pans.

> On her journey, Pop-pank would have seen buffalo herds that stretched from one side of the horizon to the other. At that time there were millions in North America. A hundred years later, whites had hunted the buffalo almost to extinction to starve out their Indian enemies.

But Pop-pank did it. She made it across North Dakota and Montana alone. Sometime that winter, she crossed the snow-covered mountains between Montana and Idaho (the same mountains that nearly killed several men in the Lewis and Clark group). Less than a year after her capture, the determined girl made it back to her village. She was home. The Shoshoni were so surprised and delighted by her courage and miraculous return that they gave her a new name—*Pop-pank*, or Jumping Fish—because of the way she raced through the stream during the Minnetare raid. She was a hero, and her story was told for years to come.

In 1805, four years later, the Lewis and Clark expedition arrived in Shoshoni country. The Indians were shocked to see the white men's pale skin. But Pop-pank was even more shocked when a young Indian woman stepped out from the crowd of men. It was her friend Sacagawea! Captain Lewis described their reunion:

> *The meeting of those people was really affecting, particularly between Sah cah-gar-we-ah and an Indian woman, who had been taken prisoner at the same time with her, and who had afterwards escaped from the Minnetares and rejoined her nation.*[5]

The two girls hadn't seen each other in years and hadn't expected to ever see each other again. They had a lot of catching up to do.

After a great deal of laughing and crying, they shared their stories. Pop-pank finally heard the strange path her friend's life had taken. After living with Charbonneau for years, Sacagawea had met Lewis and Clark. The explorers were looking for someone to guide them to the Shoshoni, the only friendly Indians who would sell them horses so they could make it to the Columbia River and the end of their journey. They realized that Sacagawea would be an invaluable guide and translator, since she was practically the only person who had been west, and she spoke the Shoshoni language. Against their better judgment, they also brought along Charbonneau, who lacked any needed skills.

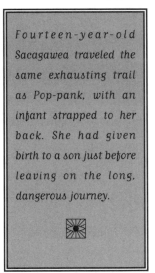

Fourteen-year-old Sacagawea traveled the same exhausting trail as Pop-pank, with an infant strapped to her back. She had given birth to a son just before leaving on the long, dangerous journey.

Each girl survived her share of amazing adventures during the last four years. But after their brief reconnection, their lives would again take different paths. Lewis and Clark's party stayed with the Shoshoni for a few weeks, but after buying horses they left to continue their journey to the Pacific. Sacagawea left with them. She never returned to her people. Pop-pank, on the other hand, a survivor and hero who risked her life to return to her nation, never left the Shoshoni again.

How Will You Rock the World?

"On TV I hear about oil spills, fires and all the animals that die from them. I will rock the world by being an environmentalist. I will go to school and learn all I can about animals so I can help."

Stephanie Robbins, age 10

"I will rock the world with my running and raising money in charity races. I already run cross-country, in 5-10k races, and for good causes like breast cancer and arthritis research, and food banks. I like running because it clears my head, helps me concentrate, and allows me to help people."

Sarah Gibbons, age 12

The Brontë Sisters

1816–1855 (Charlotte), 1818–1848 (Emily),
1820–1849 (Anne) ⊕ Authors ⊕ England

No coward soul is mine

No trembler in the world's storm-troubled sphere

I see heaven's glories shine

And Faith shines equal arming me from fear.

— a poem by Emily Brontë, from the sisters' first published book of poetry

There was a quiet knock at the bedroom door. Charlotte and Emily, who were already tucked in and reading by lantern light, looked up from their books with surprise. Who could it be so late at night? Their wild brother Branwell burst into the room. "Look what Papa has brought me!" he cried, handing them a small box. They opened the lid, and to their delight, they found a whole troop of brightly painted, wooden soldiers!

Charlotte grabbed one from the box and proclaimed, "This shall be the Duke!" Emily took another tiny soldier, crying, "This one shall be mine. He is rather grave looking, so let us call him 'Gravey'!" Their youngest sister, Anne, heard the commotion from her room and came running. She, too, chose a soldier for herself, which they named "Waiting Boy." A thousand stories swirled in their heads—dragons, castles, grand adventures and great dangers. At that moment the three sisters began creating the magical world of Gondal. All alone in their spooky, lonely house, they dreamed of becoming famous writers.

The girlhood dreams of the Brontë sisters came true beyond their wildest fantasies, but at a high cost. All three sisters published successful novels that became classics of literature, and they were sensational stars in their day. Yet their world was overshadowed by tragedy and unhappiness.

The three famous Brontë sisters, Charlotte, Emily, and Anne, originally came from a family of six children. They had two older sisters, Maria and Elizabeth, and a brother, Branwell. Just after baby Anne was born, the family moved to Haworth, a cold, wet, industrial town in northern England, where their father, the Reverend Patrick Brontë, had gotten a job. Behind their new house were the wild and windy moors, and in front stood the church and the cemetery. Their windows looked out over a sea of gravestones—perhaps a sign of the sorrows to come.

Haworth had no sewers and very polluted water, so it wasn't surprising that almost half the children born there died before turning six and the average age of death in town was just twenty-five years old! Soon after the Brontës moved there, their mother died. The children were left in the care of their eccentric father. Mr. Brontë loved his children and taught them literature, history and geography, and he held weekly discussions on politics, poetry, and literature. But he also kept them isolated from the rest of the town.

Fortunately, the children had their books, their imaginations, and most important of all, their pens. Charlotte wrote: "The liveliest pleasure we had . . . lay in attempts at literary composition." They entertained themselves by writing poems, stories, and even a monthly magazine. Their lonely house, the graveyard, the mysterious moors—all worked their way into the sisters' writing.

But Mr. Brontë began worrying about the sisters' futures. He realized that their only career option would be teaching. For that, they would need more education. When he sent Maria, Charlotte, Elizabeth, and Emily off to a boarding school, he had no idea of the nightmare he had committed them to. The girls were tormented by the terrible food, bitter cold, cruel teachers, and boring lessons. Worse yet, in 1825, a tuberculosis epidemic swept through the unsanitary school, and Maria (age eleven) and Elizabeth (age ten) died within months of each other. Charlotte and Emily were devastated and returned to the safety of their home.

Once again, the girls studied around the kitchen table. In 1826, when Branwell received his toy soldiers, the children began creating a world of stories around them. For the next five years the girls, who were ten, eight and six, wrote their tales in tiny, handmade books that were just 2 inches (5 centimeters) tall (exactly the right size for the toy soldiers), in teeny-tiny handwriting that only they could read. In one year alone, they wrote eighteen of their tiny books!

Charlotte caused a scandal when she exposed the crimes of her childhood school in her novel Jane Eyre.

Like the characters in her books, Charlotte was strong-willed. At twelve, she vowed never to marry, so she could devote her life to writing, and, at fourteen, she had already written twenty-two manuscripts! After a few more years at a new school, where she blossomed into a star student, Charlotte returned home at sixteen to teach her younger siblings and continue writing.

When she began showing her work to people outside her family, the reviews were not encouraging. She wrote to Robert Southey, a famous poet, asking for advice and enclosing some poems. He wrote back, "Literature cannot be the business of a woman's life, and it ought not to be." But Charlotte refused to let Southey's attitude discourage her—she wrote sixty more poems that year. She turned down all marriage proposals to write. Her younger sisters were inspired and started to take their own writing more seriously.

While struggling to get published, the girls had to work as teachers and governesses. They hated it. In 1845, Charlotte read some of her sisters' poetry. It was fantastic! She convinced them they should publish a book of verse together. They paid to have the book published, but had to call themselves Currer, Ellis, and Acton Bell, to avoid the prejudice against women writers. It didn't do them much good, however. Although the book got great reviews, it sold only two copies!

Undaunted, they turned their energy back to their stories, working together and reading their tales aloud to each other. Out of this collaboration came

Emily's *Wuthering Heights*, Anne's *Agnes Grey*, and Charlotte's *The Professor*. The three novels were sent off to various publishers, again using the male names, and after a year of waiting, *Wuthering Heights* and *Agnes Grey* were accepted for publication. *The Professor* was rejected everywhere.

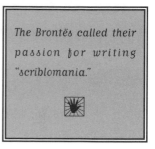

The Brontës called their passion for writing "scriblomania."

Again, Charlotte refused to be discouraged by other people's opinions and immediately started another novel. From her own experiences, Charlotte crafted *Jane Eyre*, the story of a rebellious governess who refuses to accept her "station" in life. When her manuscript reached the publishing offices of Smith, Elder & Co., it was passed around to several editors. They all loved it. One of the owners, George Smith, took it home with him; he couldn't put it down and read the entire 500-page novel in one sitting! Charlotte would finally be a published writer like her sisters.

Jane Eyre was an instant hit, praised for its original voice and fascinating story. It was also strongly criticized. People at that time weren't used to strong, passionate heroines, attacks on church hypocrisy, or the idea of equal rights for all people, regardless of their class or sex.

Wuthering Heights was equally controversial for Emily's descriptions of passionate love. When it first came out, it wasn't as successful as *Jane Eyre*, but it eventually became one of the most popular novels of all time. One critic describes it as ". . . perhaps the most passionately original novel in the English language."

Agnes Grey was well-received, but Anne's second book, *The Tenant of Wildfell Hall*, was a controversy. It was a feminist story, attacking marriage laws and the different rules men and women had to obey. Critics were so alarmed that they cautioned young ladies not to read any of the books written by the "Bell brothers."

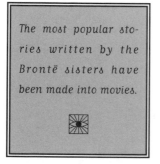

The most popular stories written by the Brontë sisters have been made into movies.

As praise and criticism for these revolutionary books grew, so did curiosity about the authors. The public wondered if they were really men, or if the novels were actually written by just one person. To quell the growing rumors, Charlotte and Anne went to London in 1848 and met with their publishers face to face for the first time. George

Smith was amazed that such powerful novels came from the minds of these petite, quiet, shy young women. When the news got out, the Brontë sisters became even more of a sensation than before.

They had made it! But real life for the Brontës took a turn for the worse. Their brother, who was never successful, drank heavily and abused drugs. Like his sisters Maria and Elizabeth, he caught tuberculosis and died in September 1848. By December, Emily had also contracted the illness, and died at age thirty. Just when Charlotte thought she could endure no more heartache, her baby sister Anne caught the same deadly disease and died the following spring, at just twenty-eight years old. In less than a year, Charlotte had lost her three remaining siblings and was left alone with her father. Of this time, she wrote in a letter to a friend, "Why life is so blank, brief and bitter, I do not know."

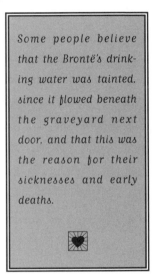

Some people believe that the Brontë's drinking water was tainted, since it flowed beneath the graveyard next door, and that this was the reason for their sicknesses and early deaths.

For the next six years, Charlotte cared for her father, taking pleasure only from her writing. She published two more popular novels, *Shirley* and *Villette*, but felt something was missing from her life. In 1854, Arthur Nicholls, a man she had already rejected, didn't give up and asked Charlotte again to be his wife. She wasn't exactly in love with him, but she knew he was kind and had a great sense of humor—something she could use after all her tragedy.

She said yes, and in June of 1854 they were married. In just a few months she grew to love her husband deeply and was happier than she'd ever been in her life. At the age of thirty-nine she became pregnant. But again, her happiness was not to last long. A few months later, she and the baby died from complications.

Three lonely sisters, with little formal education, cooped up in a strange house on the remote moors, published three of the most thrilling novels of the day. While their novels were considered strange, brutish, feminist, and revolutionary 150 years ago, they are loved today as some of the most powerful, ground-breaking stories of all time. Along with Shakespeare, Chaucer, and Dickens, the names of these sisters—Charlotte, Emily, and Anne—have gone down in history as three of the most talented authors ever.

Do you think because I am poor; obscure, plain and little, I am soulless and heartless?—You think wrong! I have as much soul as you,—and full as much heart! ... It is my spirit that addresses your spirit; just as if both had passed through the grave, and we stood at God's feet, equal—as we are!

— from *Jane Eyre*

How Will You Rock the World?

"My dream is to become a fabulous writer, no matter if I do it as a newspaper reporter or as a novelist. It doesn't matter if people know my name or if I make a lot of money; just as

long as I got my point across and people relate to and react to my stories ... maybe they'll even recall a passage I wrote. After all, that's what writing is all about."

Lauren Hart, age 13

"My dream is to become a writer. I want people to see things through my eyes— the eyes of a teen girl. I'm absolutely

not going to write about the latest teen fashions or secret crushes. I'm not into that—I want to make a difference in people's lives."

Laura DiVeglia, age 13

Clara Schumann

1819–1896 ❋ *PIANIST/COMPOSER* ❋ *GERMANY*

She plays with as much strength as six boys.
— writer Johann von Goethe, complimenting 12-year-old Clara.

Clara peeked through the doorway and gulped. The concert hall was packed with Leipzig's highest society. The candles in the chandeliers blazed and the buzz of conversations filled the air. Clara couldn't believe she would be playing for all these people. Her father found her and scolded, "Come, Clara, it's time to go on!"

As she walked out to her piano, she could hear the whispers—"Why, she's just a *child*." "Her hands are so *tiny!*" "Can she *really* play?" But as soon as Clara's fingers touched the keys, the whispers stopped. The audience sat entranced, listening to the incredible melodies of this nine-year-old genius. For Clara, everything but the piano was a blur. All she knew were the keys and her music. It wasn't until she finished her pieces that she noticed the audience again. For a moment they were silent—dumbstruck. Then the delighted crowd erupted into loud applause. In Clara's first public performance, she took her city by storm—as she would the rest of Europe in the following years.

Clara Wieck was destined to become a world-famous pianist. She was born in Leipzig, Germany to two of its most famous musicians. Her mother, Marianne, was a popular singer, and her father, Frederick, an acclaimed piano teacher. Clara grew up surrounded by music; the sounds of her father's piano and her mother's voice were her lullabies.

Clara's parents may have been a good musical match, but emotionally, their marriage was a wreck. When they divorced, Clara's tyrannical father took the children—divorced women had virtually no rights back then, so Marianne had to give them up. Clara withdrew from her unhappy surroundings. She did not speak or respond to other people's words for many years. Because she lived in her own inner world, many people thought she was deaf or mentally retarded. When her father began teaching her to play the piano, at age five, he was surprised to find she had no problems hearing *music*. As her musical abilities improved, so did her hearing and speech.

At a time when most girls received little or no education, Frederick insisted on strenuous studies for Clara. On top of hours of daily piano lessons, Clara attended the opera, concerts, and the theater with her father, and studied reading, writing, music theory, music composition, French, English, and religion. Frederick quickly realized he had a child prodigy on his hands. Clara could listen to a piano piece just once and play it back flawlessly, without seeing any written music. She could play difficult pieces better than most adults, with genuine emotion and her own personal style. Her father decided she was ready for her first public performance when she was just nine years old.

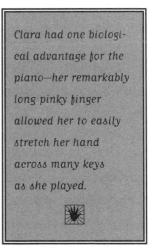

Clara had one biological advantage for the piano—her remarkably long pinky finger allowed her to easily stretch her hand across many keys as she played.

He arranged for Clara to play at the Gewandhaus, the most important concert hall in Leipzig. Famous musicians from all over the world played there—including Clara's own mother. Clara was thrilled. She surprised and impressed the sophisticated audience and the critics, who wrote:

It was especially pleasing to hear the young, musically talented
Clara Wiek [sic], just nine years old, perform . . . to universal and
well-earned applause . . . We may entertain the greatest hopes for
this child . . .[6]

With this great success, Frederick began scheduling concerts for Clara all over Europe. She played the popular music of the day, plus pieces she wrote herself. In Dresden, she entertained royal families and won their hearts with her charm and talent. In Paris, the music center of the world, she was such a hit that critics wrote of one performance:

. . . the artist, who is still so young received thunderous applause . . .
the great skill, assurance, and strength with which she plays even
the most difficult movements is highly remarkable. Even more
remarkable is the spirit and feeling of her performance; one could
scarcely wish for more.[7]

And in Vienna, Austria, she was so beloved that the Emperor himself gave her the title of "Royal and Imperial Virtuoso." Her father wrote in a letter home, "All Vienna is saying that no artist has ever made a sensation like this . . . now the whole world shall know there is only one Clara." Over the years she became one of the most popular pianists, man or woman, in all of Europe and began earning a great deal of money.

Just as Clara's fame was skyrocketing, she met a young man who would change her life forever. In 1828, the year Clara played her first concert, eighteen-year-old Robert Schumann began studying with her father. Frederick was reluctant to take on such an old student, but he saw some promise in Robert, who moved into their home for intensive training. Robert wasn't as good on the piano as young Clara, but he had a gift for writing music. It wasn't until years after his death that Robert Schumann would be recognized as one of the greatest composers of all time.

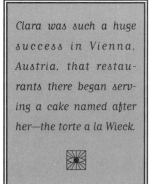

Clara was such a huge success in Vienna. Austria. that restaurants there began serving a cake named after her—the torte a la Wieck.

For Clara, Robert was a breath of fresh air after years with her demanding father. For Robert, Clara was an inspiration, not to mention a great help to his career. She loved performing his compositions and helped popularize his music with her fans. Robert and Clara spent years as friends and music partners, but by the time she was sixteen, their relationship had changed. They were madly in love. In 1840, the day before Clara's twenty-first birthday, they were finally married, against Frederick's wishes. He didn't speak to them for years.

Clara was an independent woman and planned to continue performing after her marriage. But it wasn't that easy. She was often pregnant, giving birth to eight children in ten years. Her husband was also challenging. Robert's genius was not recognized during his lifetime, and he struggled with his wife's greater fame. He was miserable when he toured with her and she got all the attention, but when she went without him, it was even worse. During one of her trips, he wrote, "Have you forgotten me already? Letting you go was one of the most foolish things I ever did in my life and it certainly won't happen again." He also resented that Clara was the family's only breadwinner.

When Robert asked to marry Clara, her father said no, and threatened to shoot Robert if he ever saw him again. The couple didn't see or speak to each other for almost two years, until they convinced the courts to let them marry without parental approval.

While Clara lived with her father, he gave her almost none of the money she was paid for her countless performances. Later, she actually had to sue him to reclaim some of her vast earnings.

By 1854, Robert was overcome by depression. He tried to kill himself and was committed to a mental institution. The doctors let Clara see him only once, and, two years later, he died. From then on, Clara worked very hard to support her children. She toured almost non-stop. Although raising and supporting her children alone was difficult, Clara took comfort in her art. She wrote, "Work is always the best diversion from pain."

For forty-five years after Robert died, Clara performed to adoring crowds all over Europe. Her career lasted longer than almost any other musician of her time, and by the time she died, at age seventy-seven, Clara had played over 1,300 performances! She was also a talented composer whose works are still played today.

But Clara's legacy goes well beyond her own piano playing. She also influenced some of the greatest composers of the 19th century. Paganini, Chopin, Mendelssohn, Schumann, Lizst, and Brahms all looked to Clara as a teacher, friend and inspiration. While they were unknown, Clara offered to play their music. She played it brilliantly and helped make many composers into legends. Clara had a gift for the piano, it is true, but it is how she used this gift to overcome a difficult childhood, cope with a tough marriage, help struggling young composers and support her family for fifty years, that is the real story of her greatness.

> *I always pray to God to give me the strength to successfully over-*
> *come the frightful agitations that I have lived through . . . My true*
> *old friend, my piano, must help me with this! . . . all my pain and*
> *joy can be relieved only by divine music.*
>
> — Clara Schumann

How Will You Rock the World?

"I will rock the world by being the best violin and piano player ever. I want people to be happy when they hear my music."

Rose-Claire Guthrie, age 10

Harriet Tubman

1820–1913 ❧ *ABOLITIONIST* ❧ *UNITED STATES*

*There was one or two things
I had a right to, liberty or
death. If I could not have
one, I would have the other,
for no man should take me
alive. I should fight for my
liberty as long as my
strength lasted.*

— Harriet Tubman

H arriet stood in the hot sun, shucking corn with the rest of the slaves. Out of the corner of her eye she noticed a tall black man slip into the woods. Her heart raced! Was he running away? Harriet had always dreamed of running away. Worry gnawed at her heart—would he make it? Kicking up a cloud of dust, the overseer galloped past, pulling out his snakeskin whip as he neared the woods. He was after the slave! She had to do something, but what? What could a fifteen-year-old black girl do to stop a white man?

Without thinking, Harriet took off after them. She caught up at the plantation store, where the overseer was holding onto the slave. Harriet recognized the terror in the black man's eyes. When the overseer spotted her, he yelled, "You. Hold this man while I tie him for his lashing." In a quiet, angry voice, Harriet replied, "No, I won't." He was so stunned by her words that he lost his grip on the slave, who bolted from the store. Before you could blink, Harriet moved so she stood in the door, blocking the white man from chasing the slave. In his rage, the overseer grabbed a lead weight and hurled it toward the escaping slave, but he missed. The weight hit young Harriet right between the eyes. Blood gushed from the wound and the world went dark.

It was the first time this fifteen-year-old girl helped one of her people run toward freedom and took the beating for it, but it certainly was not her last. In just a few years Harriet would have a new name—one that would be praised by blacks and feared by white slave owners—"Moses," after the Jewish hero who led his people out of slavery in Egypt. Harriet "Moses" Tubman would lead more blacks out of slavery than any other person, male or female, black or white, in American history.

> *Harriet's bravery should come as no surprise: her parents were of the Ashanti people. These fierce warriors lived in West Africa, where they successfully fought off British invasion during the 1800s.*
>
>

Harriet was born into slavery sometime in 1820 (no one bothered to keep track of slaves' birthdays), on a plantation in Maryland. She was one of the eleven children of Harriet Green and Benjamin Ross. Her parents, who couldn't marry because it was illegal for slaves, were brought to the plantation from Africa in chains. Her mother worked in the "big house," and her father cut wood for their white master, Mr. Brodas.

Brodas made much of his fortune from renting out his slaves, but also from breeding and selling them, like animals. As a young girl, Harriet saw many of her siblings and friends "sold down the river," never to be seen again. Her worst nightmare was to be sold to another plantation further south, far from her parents and friends. Harriet always dreamed of running away to the North, where she would be free.

Slaves didn't get to be kids for long. When Harriet was just five, her master rented her out to work for a local family. She slept on the kitchen floor and shared scraps with the dog for meals! Harriet hated working inside, near her white captors, so she convinced her master that she was better outdoors. When he witnessed her unusual strength, Brodas quickly put her to work with the men, plowing, chopping wood, and driving oxen. Harriet considered the hard labor an improvement, but never lost sight of her dreams of freedom.

But getting to freedom was not easy. When a master reported a runaway slave, groups of white trackers searched the surrounding countryside with dogs. If caught, a runaway would be whipped, branded (like cattle) with the letter *R*, and sent to the dreaded Deep South, where treatment of slaves was horrific. Harriet's back was already crisscrossed with scars from her many whippings, so she wasn't afraid.

Harriet first helped a runaway slave when she was just fifteen, and the blow she took from the overseer almost killed her. She was in a coma for weeks, and it would be over six months before she could walk again. For the rest of her life, she was scarred by an ugly dent in her forehead and suffered "sleeping fits." Several times a day, no matter where she was or what she was doing, Harriet would suddenly drop into a deep sleep from which no one could wake her until she regained consciousness on her own. In spite of her wounds, Harriet never regretted her act of rebellion.

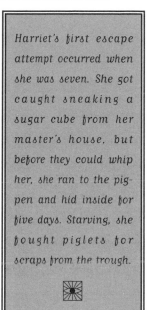

Harriet's first escape attempt occurred when she was seven. She got caught sneaking a sugar cube from her master's house, but before they could whip her, she ran to the pigpen and hid inside for five days. Starving, she fought piglets for scraps from the trough.

Her master, however, was not pleased, and decided it was time to sell his troublesome slave. Even while Harriet was lying in a coma, he brought prospective buyers in to look at her. As she recovered, Harriet prayed, "Oh dear Lord, change that man's heart . . ." When that appeal didn't work, she switched tactics, "Lord, if you're never going to change that man's heart, *kill* him . . ." Soon after she made her pleas, Mr. Brodas fell ill and died, but his successor still planned to sell Harriet, so she got ready to escape.

Harriet had heard tales of the underground railroad—a network of people willing to hide runaway slaves in their homes and help them as they journeyed north to freedom. By night, slaves walked and hid in wagons, boats, and trains. By day, they slept in safe stations—houses, churches, and barns—whose owners supported freedom for blacks. Harriet could read a compass and planned to use the railroad to make it to the free states.

One dark night in 1849, Harriet finally set out alone. At the first station she was given slips of paper with names of friendly families up the road. At these houses, Harriet presented her "tickets" and was allowed in. At one house they gave her a broom and told her to sweep the porch. She was upset until she realized that this was their way of hiding her—no one would question a black woman sweeping. Traveling by night, Harriet trudged through 90 miles (145 km) of swamp and woods until she finally crossed into free Pennsylvania. Of her first taste of liberty, she said:

> *I looked at my hands to see if I was the same person now that I was free. There was such a glory over everything; the sun came like gold through the trees, and over the fields, and I felt like I was in heaven.*[8]

But Harriet wasn't satisfied with just her own freedom. She worried about her family, friends and others still living in bondage. She immediately began planning her first rescue mission. From 1850 to 1860, she made nineteen risky trips back into the South, "conducting" 300 runaway slaves north to freedom.

Harriet always gave herself a head start on the whites. She arrived at plantations late Saturday night, disguised as an old woman, then led groups out on Sunday, knowing owners wouldn't chase them that day. She was also remarkably cool-headed on those long, treacherous journeys north and discouraged fear in her "passengers." If a runaway got scared and wanted to turn back (which would endanger the entire underground railroad), Harriet put her pistol to the runaway's head and said, "Move or die." It worked. In ten years, Harriet never lost a single "passenger."

Harriet even snuck back to the Brodas plantation, where her chances of being recognized and caught were terribly high. By 1857, she had rescued her entire family, including her elderly parents.

> *Once Harriet and her "passengers" hid in a pile of manure, breathing through straws!*

At first Harriet led her escaped slaves to the northern states of the U.S., but this became too dangerous when Congress passed the Fugitive Slave Law in 1850, demanding the return of escaped slaves and punishing those who helped them. Harriet refused to give up, and, instead, led her people all the way to Canada. It turned a 90-mile (145-km) escape route into a 500-mile (800-km) one, but at least the ex-slaves knew they would be truly free.

The mysterious thief angered and scared white plantation owners, who just assumed that "Moses" was a man. How could a woman—a black woman, at that—be so cunning and bold as to steal slaves right from under their noses? The usual reward for catching a slave ranged from a hundred to a thousand dollars, but slave owners put an amazing reward on "Moses'" head—*forty thousand* dollars! Though the South swarmed with bounty hunters, they never caught Harriet as she freed slave after slave.

When the Civil War broke out in 1860, many Southern slaves fled their masters and ran to the Union troops, who unfortunately weren't prepared to deal with them. From her home in Canada, Harriet traveled to South Carolina and worked as a nurse on the front lines, caring for both black "freed men" and white soldiers.

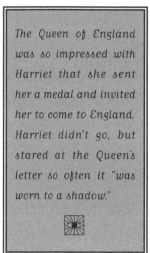

The Queen of England was so impressed with Harriet that she sent her a medal and invited her to come to England. Harriet didn't go, but stared at the Queen's letter so often it "was worn to a shadow."

Harriet was soon recruited as a spy because of her extensive knowledge of the Southern states and her legendary courage. She led groups of black soldiers into enemy territory, informing Union officers about the actions of Confederate troops and the locations of ammunition depots and slaves waiting to be freed. Union General Rufus Saxton praised her: "She made many a raid inside the enemy's lines, displaying remarkable courage, zeal, and fidelity." In one legendary raid, Harriet and 150 black soldiers attacked a Confederate outpost in South Carolina and freed 750 slaves! What sweet revenge for Harriet and her men.

After the war, Harriet settled in Auburn, New York, a former station on the underground railroad, to care for her elderly parents. Never one to miss out on any excitement, in 1870, fifty-year-old Harriet fell in love with a man in his twenties! She married Nelson Davis, a Civil War veteran, and became a popular and moving speaker on the rights of blacks and women.

Despite her fame and all she had accomplished, Harriet was practically penniless after the war. She and friends wrote to the U.S. government to pay her a pension, just like it paid to male soldiers who had served in the Civil War. No luck. When her husband died at forty-four (Yes, Harriet outlived her young husband!), the government paid her an $8 monthly pension as his widow, but still didn't recognize her for her own service!

Harriet's dream in her old age was to build a home for sick and elderly ex-slaves, a place where they would be safe and taken care of after all their struggles. Out of the money earned from sales of her biography, Harriet was finally able to build her retirement home in 1908, and at age eighty-eight, she was one of the first to move in. Five years later, surrounded by her friends and family, and in the home she built from her dreams, Harriet finally quit the struggle and died of pneumonia at the age of ninety-three.

In Cambridge, Maryland, not far from where Harriet lived in slavery, Tubman Street reminds us of the girl who refused to accept her lot in life. When up against the foreboding wall of slavery, the woman they called "Moses" persevered, risking her life again and again to help others and lead her people to freedom.

> *Oh go down, Moses,*
> *Way down in Egypt land,*
> *Tell old Pharaoh,*
> *Let my people go.*
> — a song Harriet sang as she led slaves to freedom.

How Will You Rock the World?

"I want to see women in the workforce make exactly as much as men. I will work for an end to the exploitation of and violence against women. I would like to see changes in the U.S. Constitution to better protect women, children and people of color."

Margaret Hill Argenzio, age 9

Florence Nightingale

1820–1910 ✤ Nurse ✤ England

What a comfort it was to see her pass. We lay there by the hundreds. But we could kiss her shadow as it fell and lay our heads on the pillow again, content.
— a wounded soldier praising the "Lady with the Lamp"

F lorence walked down the dark hall of the British hospital. The floors and walls were disgusting; they looked like they'd never seen a good scrubbing. And what was that foul smell? When she turned a corner, Florence could see a stream of blood and human waste flowing down the middle of the hall and emptying into an open drain. She plugged her nose, covered her mouth, and continued on.

She could hear horrible cries and moans through each doorway, and when she peeked her head into a room, she saw a filthy man lying in a bed that looked like it hadn't been changed for weeks. The poor soul was being tormented by a cloud of flies that was attracted to the stench.

Florence was horrified. "Nurse, nurse!" she cried. And when the "nurse" finally staggered into the room, Florence could see that the woman was no nurse at all—and she was drunk! Florence couldn't believe her eyes. It was no wonder so many people died in hospitals! Everywhere she looked she saw things that could be improved, but no one seemed to care. These were just poor people, after all.

But Florence cared. She dedicated her life not only to comforting the sick, but also to reforming hospitals and the profession of nursing. She completely reinvented the way hospitals were run and how the sick were cared for. The kind-hearted "Lady with the Lamp" became a legend in her own time, and is now recognized as the founder of modern nursing.

Florence and her older sister were educated at home by their father. While Florence was an intelligent student, she was also quite pretty and was expected to make a good marriage. Florence, however, had other plans. Even as a young girl, she felt the life of a wealthy English woman was boring and pointless. She wanted to do something meaningful. In 1837, the rebellious sixteen-year-old heard the voice of God speak to her, calling her to do good works. At the time, she wasn't sure exactly what "good works" she should do, but she began visiting the sick in local villages, bringing them food and changing their bedding.

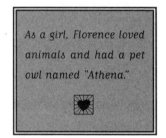

As a girl, Florence loved animals and had a pet owl named "Athena."

Her parents disapproved. It was "unladylike." When Florence asked to visit hospitals to learn more about nursing, her parents were horrified! Hospitals were for poor people who couldn't afford to be cared for at home. They were certainly no place for a beautiful, wealthy bride-to-be. Florence defied her parents and followed her calling.

Indeed, English hospitals were worse than Florence had ever imagined. The nurses were uneducated, poorly paid, and often drunk. It's not surprising that they neglected patients and treated them cruelly. Diseases spread quickly in the filthy, overcrowded rooms. In fact, at the time, anyone who actually went into a hospital could expect to die, rather than get better. Florence began studying the problems, writing to experts around the world, and formulating her own ideas for improvements.

During this busy time in her life, Florence was also being pursued by one of the most eligible bachelors in England, Richard Milnes. She actually cared strongly for Richard and even wanted to marry him, but knew that it would destroy her chances of pursuing a nursing career.

When Florence finally rejected him and vowed to never marry, she became quite depressed. To help cheer her up and, at the same time, distract her from her nursing passion, Florence's parents sent her off to tour Europe. Instead of changing her mind, however, the trip actually strengthened Florence's resolve. She studied how the sick were cared for in Italy, Egypt, Greece, and, finally, in Germany, where she visited an innovative hospital and nursing school. She saw that when patients were clean, well-fed, and taken care of, they recovered more quickly.

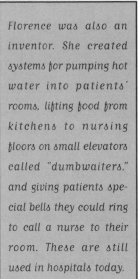

Florence was also an inventor. She created systems for pumping hot water into patients' rooms, lifting food from kitchens to nursing floors on small elevators called "dumbwaiters," and giving patients special bells they could ring to call a nurse to their room. These are still used in hospitals today.

When Florence returned to England, she shocked her parents by packing up and moving out. She went back to the German nursing school, where she trained for four months, then finished up her studies in Paris, where exciting discoveries were being made about germs and how disease is spread. By 1853, thirty-three-year-old Florence was appointed superintendent of a women's hospital in London, where she was able to put her theories into practice. Florence's improvements were very successful and her reputation grew. Her dreams were finally coming true!

In 1854, England entered the Crimean War (in present-day Turkey) and suffered heavy casualties. When newspapers reported on the terrible medical facilities for wounded soldiers, it caused an uproar in England. The government recruited Florence to go to the battle area and try to improve conditions. She took thirty-eight nurses, and set off for the front lines of the war.

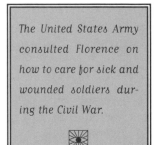

The United States Army consulted Florence on how to care for sick and wounded soldiers during the Civil War.

Conditions were far worse than the papers had reported. The nurses arrived at a war hospital in Turkey to find thousands of soldiers lying on straw in the hallways, covered with their own blood and excrement. Everything was crawling with fleas and rats. There were no beds, soap, blankets or clean clothing, not even enough water for the injured men. At night, the injured and dying men were left alone in the terrifying darkness.

To Florence's surprise, the army officers were not happy to see the nurses; they resented being told what to do by women. So Florence did the work without their help. There were no funds for supplies, so Florence used her own money. The nurses cleaned the hospital and the men, and even brought in a sanitary team to drain the cesspool that the hospital was built on. They set up a kitchen and made sure the wounded soldiers were well-fed. They comforted the men by reading to them and writing their letters home.

Each night Florence lit her lantern and made her rounds, giving comfort and advice to the frightened men. When they saw her light coming down the hall, the men instantly felt that everything would be okay. The grateful soldiers began calling her "The Lady with the Lamp."

Miraculously, the death rate at the hospital dropped from 42% to 2% in just 5 months! With her renovation of the hospital complete, Florence turned her attention to improving the entire army medical system. She sent plans back to England for reorganizing all military hospitals, keeping military medical records, and establishing an army medical school to train doctors and nurses in techniques and medicines specific to the battlefield.

When the war ended in 1856 and Florence returned home, she was a hero. She was such a success that the public raised money for Florence to continue her reforms in the hospitals of England. She was invited to meet with Queen Victoria to discuss further improvements. The Queen set up a Royal Commission to decide on Florence's suggestions, and, before long, England had its first Army Medical School, greatly improved army barracks and hospitals, and the best army medical records in Europe.

Sadly, either the mental or physical strain of the war seemed to have ruined Florence's health. Four months after returning to England, she hid herself away, never appearing or speaking in public again. In fact, for much of the next fifty years Florence didn't even leave her bed. But this didn't stop her from working.

She continued to campaign for improved health standards around the world, publishing over 200 books and reports. In 1860, her book,

Some people think Florence suffered from Post-Traumatic Stress Disorder after the Crimean war, and this is what kept her bedridden for the rest of her life. PTSD is now an accepted mental disorder that usually affects soldiers who have been exposed to trauma during a war.

Notes on Nursing, was first published. Since then it has sold millions of copies, been translated into dozens of languages, and is still in print today. That same year, Florence used the money raised by the public to found the Nightingale Training School for Nurses in London—the only school of its kind in the world. Graduates of the school went to work in British hospitals and abroad, establishing the "Nightingale Model" worldwide.

For the rest of her long life (she lived to be ninety), Florence was sought after by governments all over the world for her advice on nursing, hospitals and sanitation. Her farsighted reforms changed the very nature of modern health care and saved countless lives. Even today, "The Lady with the Lamp" continues to inspire nurses, doctors, and health care workers around the world.

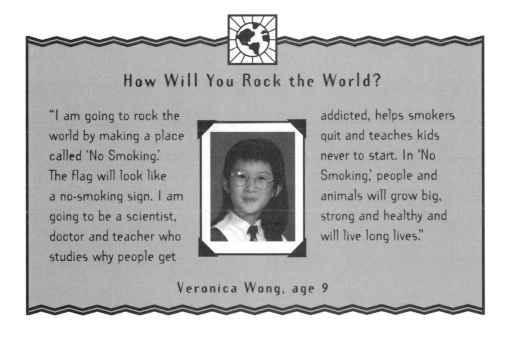

How Will You Rock the World?

"I am going to rock the world by making a place called 'No Smoking.' The flag will look like a no-smoking sign. I am going to be a scientist, doctor and teacher who studies why people get addicted, helps smokers quit and teaches kids never to start. In 'No Smoking,' people and animals will grow big, strong and healthy and will live long lives."

Veronica Wong, age 9

Margaret Knight

1838–1914 ✸ *INVENTOR* ✸ *UNITED STATES*

I sighed sometimes, because I was not like other girls; but wisely concluded that I couldn't help it, and sought further consolation from my tools.
— Margaret Knight

T he whirring and clicking of the machines hummed in Margaret's ears, almost hypnotizing her as she worked. Suddenly, the loom next to hers began making strange noises and before she could react, it went haywire. The heavy spindle flew off and its steel-tipped needle plunged into her neighbor's leg. Margaret stared in shock—blood was everywhere. The mill erupted in chaos that didn't stop until the screaming girl was carted off to the hospital. When things calmed down and people went fearfully back to work, Margaret couldn't get the image out of her mind. There had to be a way to automatically shut off a loom when it malfunctioned, so the spindle wouldn't fly off and injure the worker. But how?

It's a wonder that twelve-year-old Margaret ever solved this riddle. She lived in a time when a woman was more likely to sprout wings than become an inventor. Victorian girls were raised to be good wives and mothers, nothing more. They were taught to bake, sew and clean house rather than work with tools and other "manly interests." And yet, from her earliest memories, Margaret was obsessed with tools, machines and how to build things. She described her unpopular interests:

> *As a child I never cared for things that girls usually do; dolls never possessed any charms for me. I couldn't see the sense of coddling bits of porcelain with senseless faces; the only things I wanted were a jack-knife, a gimlet, and pieces of wood.*9

Margaret's girlfriends in Springfield, Massachusetts, were appalled and called her "tomboy" and worse. But she didn't let them stop her creativity. The boys liked her just fine, and came around constantly begging her to make them things. She was famous in the neighborhood for the kites and sleds she built. She took a lot more pride in them than she did in her household chores.

Margaret's family was poor, so she didn't get much schooling and had to work in a cotton mill when she was young. But it was her work there that gave twelve-year-old Margaret the inspiration for her first invention. After the mill accident, she was consumed day and night until she figured out a way to shut off a malfunctioning loom. Her stop-motion device was immediately put to work at the cotton mill and then in mills all over America. A twelve-year-old's invention saved countless lives.

Margaret didn't earn any money for this invention, and spent her teen years working in various mills, in photography and engraving studios, and even repairing houses. This didn't leave much time for inventing, but Margaret constantly studied the tools and machinery she worked with, learning how they functioned and imagining how she might improve them. It was during these years that her inventions took shape in her head.

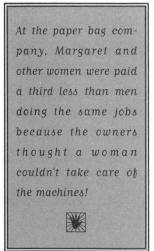

At the paper bag company, Margaret and other women were paid a third less than men doing the same jobs because the owners thought a woman couldn't take care of the machines!

Her most famous invention came to her while working at the Columbia Paper Bag Company. At the time, paper bags had to be glued together by hand. They were envelope-shaped and flimsy, usually falling apart before people could get their groceries home. Margaret devised a machine that could cut, fold, and paste the bags together without human labor. The bags it made were strong and flat-bottomed, like our grocery bags today.

She made thousands of trial bags on a wooden model before deciding to patent her invention. A patent is a document that proves a person invented something and gives that person the right to sell the idea or let others use it for a fee. Patents are how inventors make money for their ideas. Although Margaret had been inventing her entire life, she was thirty years old when she applied for her first patent. She knew her wooden model wouldn't do for the patent office, so she took it to a shop to have an iron one built. When it was finished and she applied for her patent, Margaret got the shock of her life.

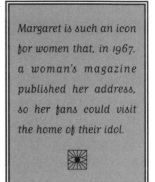

Margaret is such an icon for women that, in 1967, a woman's magazine published her address, so her fans could visit the home of their idol.

A certain Charles Annan beat her to it. He had already applied for a patent on a bag-making machine that looked just like hers! It turns out he studied her model while it was in the shop. Even though he admitted to spying, Annan claimed that he had the idea first and that no woman could possibly understand the mechanical complexities of such a machine. Margaret was outraged.

Although she knew it would be an uphill battle to fight male prejudice, she had put too much work into her invention to just give up. She scraped together all her money and paid a lawyer one hundred dollars a day to help her fight for what was hers. They called witnesses—her boss at the bag factory, the machinist who built her iron model, her roommate— who all testified that Margaret had been working on the machine years before Annan.

Margaret herself defended her mechanical abilities, "I have from my earliest recollection been connected in some way with machinery." She showed the court early sketches, notes, and photos, and she even let the judge read her diary, which was full of dreams about her precious bag machine! The judge and jury were overwhelmed with evidence that Margaret was no average lady. She won her case and her patent.

Victory was sweet, not only because Margaret had proved that a woman could invent an incredibly complex machine, but also because it was worth a fortune! She got her machines built and formed the Eastern Paper Bag Company to produce her bags. And, unlike many inventors, Margaret enjoyed the fruits of her inventing success *during* her lifetime. Her invention earned her extraordinary attention (It could do the work of thirty people!), earnings of around $50,000, and a medal from Queen Victoria!

Even though Margaret had little schooling, she taught herself everything she needed to know about patent law, contract negotiating and licensing. It was a good thing, too, because over the next forty-five years, she came up with almost ninety more inventions. She patented about twenty-five of them, including new shoe-cutting machines, window sashes, rotary engines and motors for cars. She spent almost every day in her "experiment rooms" until she died at the age of seventy-six. In the last year of her life, a *New York Times* article described her continued creativity and stamina: "Miss Margaret Knight is working twenty hours a day on her eighty-ninth invention."

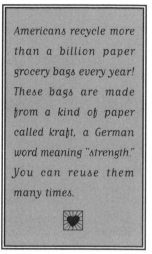

Americans recycle more than a billion paper grocery bags every year! These bags are made from a kind of paper called kraft, a German word meaning "strength." You can reuse them many times.

Margaret was one of the most productive female inventors ever. Her fame made her a role model for other girl and women inventors who followed in her footsteps. She was not only a brilliant inventor, but also a shrewd businesswoman and a real fighter when it came to protecting her ideas. Margaret never let people's prejudices about women stop her from doing what she loved—figuring out ways to make things better—and she never let anyone else take credit for her ideas!

How Will You Rock the World?

"I will rock the world by being the person who discovers the cure for AIDS and the common cold. I will either discover a vaccine or a medicine you can take by mouth."

Patricia Grinnell, age 10

"I will help the environment by cloning endangered species to make them common animals again."

Katrina Gonseth, age 12

"My friend's uncle died a year ago from cancer. I will rock the world by finding a cure for this horrible disease. I will train until my brains feel like they're going to pop! If the cure involves risking my own life, I would do it to save others. I hope that someday I help cancer disappear, like small pox."

Jen Jaffe, age 12

Anna Pavlova

1881–1931 ◈ *BALLERINA* ◈ *RUSSIA*

A gleam! a flash! a shimmering vision of beauty! Is it some creature from fairyland, some spirit of ethereal grace freed from the terrestrial trammels of the flesh? No. Merely Pavlova, the incomparable Pavlova.

— The Manchester Evening News, 1925

T he streets of St. Petersburg were covered with white snow. Everything glistened and shone under the streetlights as Anna's sleigh glided silently through the city. A snowflake landed on her nose and she and her mother laughed with happiness. They were going to the ballet. Anna had never been, but just the word "ballet" seemed full of magic to her. "You are going to see the country of the fairies," her mother whispered. Anna couldn't wait.

The Maryinsky Theatre was the most beautiful place Anna had ever seen—the blue velvet, the gold paint, the lavish gowns, the gleaming chandeliers. As soon as she heard the music of Tchaikovsky and saw the ballerinas step into their dance of *Sleeping Beauty*, Anna began to tremble. It was all so beautiful she was overwhelmed; she felt almost sick. Little Anna sat entranced until the lights came up again, and she declared excitedly to her mother, "One day I will dance by myself, like Sleeping Beauty. One day I will, and in this very theater!" Her mother laughed, but Anna knew it was the truth.

No one would have guessed that Anna would ever have the strength and stamina to become a dancer, like she dreamed. She was born prematurely, and was so small that her parents rushed to have her baptized in case she died. She surprised them and survived, but was often ill. After her father died, when Anna was two, she and her mother had very little money. Sometimes they had nothing to eat but rye bread and cabbage soup. Anna grew up under-nourished and was a skinny, sickly child.

When Anna was eight, her mother saved every penny so she could give her daughter a special treat, the night at the ballet, the night Anna found her future. Her mother was skeptical of Anna's dreams, but took her to the Imperial Ballet School to stop her pleading. When the school told Anna she was too young and would need to return and audition in two years, her mother thought that was the end of it. But not for Anna.

She spent the next two years imitating every move she saw that night at the ballet, and on her tenth birthday, she went for her audition. The examinations were difficult and competitive; about 250 children auditioned each year, but only twelve got in. Anna's two years of hard work had paid off. She was chosen. She immediately moved into the school. After a childhood of poverty, the Imperial Ballet School seemed like heaven on earth to Anna. Not only did she get three hearty meals a day, plus medical attention, but she also studied dance, piano, acting and pantomime.

After eight years of training, Anna graduated and joined the Imperial Ballet. At eighteen, she danced in her first public performance. Anna was unlike anything Russian audiences had ever seen. Tall, muscular dancers were the style of the time, while Anna was short and thin. But her unusual grace and fragile beauty set her apart, and her exquisite dancing caught everyone's attention. Within a few years she was promoted to Prima Ballerina (the ballet's star).

As Anna's popularity grew, she left St. Petersburg and danced in the major cities of Russia. Before long, requests to see this new

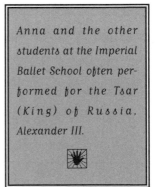

Anna and the other students at the Imperial Ballet School often performed for the Tsar (King) of Russia, Alexander III.

talent were pouring in from other countries as well, and soon, Anna was dancing all over Europe. One reviewer in London wrote of Anna's astounding popularity:

> *"Have you seen Pavlova?" The words have become almost a catch*
> *phrase. At the dinner tables or in clubs . . . the talk turns on Anna*
> *Pavlova . . . whose art is of a kind which has never before been*
> *seen in London. People go to see [her] again and again. There*
> *have been world-famous entertainers at this house before . . . but*
> *never until today has there been a sensation of the century.*[10]

Her fame spread across the Atlantic, and, in 1910, Anna sailed to America, where she made her debut at New York City's world-famous Metropolitan Opera House.

Anna loved traveling and knew she could earn a great deal more money outside of Russia. So, although the Russian Ballet offered her the highest salary in its history, in 1912, she decided to leave her home country for good. She moved to a magnificent estate in London. A woman with many dreams, Anna now had the money to realize them. She started a dance school for young girls and also formed her own dance company.

With a "family" of dancers to support, Anna and her troupe soon departed on a successful six-month tour of America. When they returned to Europe, political tension was high. Little did Anna know it would be the last time she would ever dance in Russia. The first World War was about to sweep across the continent and change life in Europe forever. Anna was performing in Berlin

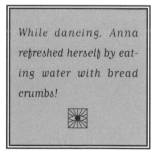

While dancing. Anna refreshed herself by eating water with bread crumbs!

when the war started, but managed to get to England on one of the last boats to cross the English Channel before war broke out! She took her company back to America, with no idea how they would support themselves while the world was at war.

Another of Anna's dreams was to expose all people, rich and poor, all over the world, to the beauty of ballet. So, over the next decade, she did her best to bring ballet to every corner of the globe, dancing in such exotic locations as Cuba, Costa Rica, Brazil, China, Japan, Indonesia, India, Egypt, and

New Zealand. Anna introduced these countries to ballet, but they introduced her to their native dances and costumes. Because of her world travels, Anna's dances became more exotic and colorful.

Many of the countries she visited didn't have appropriate theaters to host the dancers. But that didn't stop Anna. In Mexico City, she and her company danced for 30,000 fans inside a huge bullring! The heat was so intense that many of the dancers nearly passed out. Not Anna. Even when a tropical storm hit, she continued dancing in the rain until the stage became dangerously slick and they had to pull her off! The delighted crowd showered Anna with their sombreros.

Throughout her career, but especially after the horrors of World War I, Anna was extremely compassionate and generous with her talents. She often gave benefit performances to raise money for wounded soldiers, war veterans, widows, orphans, the poor and the homeless. She even adopted and raised a group of refugee girls. But her contributions never felt like enough to Anna, who said, "I can offer nothing but my art. It is a poor thing when such brave deeds are being done."

Although Anna was small, her appetite was not. One interviewer wrote, "To see the delicate, fragile Pavlova, whose waist I could span with the fingers of my two hands, attack that two-inch steak made me gasp." She even drank gallons of cod liver oil in her efforts to put on weight!

A desire to always do more drove her. In an interview she said, "I feel that, if I were ever quite satisfied, any power I possess would leave me. It is the divine discontent that drives us artists always onward." Although she had plenty of money to stop working, Anna never considered it. Even when she turned fifty years old, she would not retire. Her dedication may have hastened her death. In 1931, in between sold-out tours, Anna died from an illness made critical by her lack of rest.

In a time before airplanes and freeways, Anna traveled more than 500,000 miles, giving thousands of performances for millions of people. For most of these audiences, Anna was their first glimpse at ballet. And just as Anna the child began dreaming during her first visit to the ballet,

When she was very busy dancing, Anna would use up to 2,000 pairs of shoes a year! That's over five pairs each night!

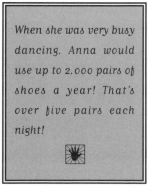

Anna the Prima Ballerina spent the rest of her life introducing people to her dream, hoping to inspire the world.

> *Dancing is my gift and my life . . . God gave me this gift to bring delight to others. I am haunted by the need to dance. It is the purest expression of every emotion, earthly and spiritual. It is happiness.*

> — Anna Pavlova

How Will You Rock the World?

"I take dance classes and think it's important for every girl to have a hobby she feels confident in. When I become  a dance instructor, I'll encourage girls to be themselves and to feel confident in what they do."

Sarah Coon, age 14

"I've been skating for over ten years! I will rock this world by  becoming the most famous figure skater in the world."

Angela Costanza, age 11

Coco Chanel

1883–1971 ✸ FASHION DESIGNER ✸ FRANCE

[Coco is] the woman with the most sense in Europe.
— Pablo Picasso

Gabrielle descended the staircase very, very carefully. Her ruffled purple velvet dress was long and heavy, and she was afraid she might trip. She couldn't wait to get to the graduation ceremony and see the looks on the faces of all her wealthy classmates. They wouldn't believe the lavish dress she had on, and they'd never guess she designed and made it herself. But it was the look on her aunt's face that caught her attention.

"What, my dear, are you *wearing*? That dress looks horrible on you! Purple is not your color at all, and I can hardly see you under all those folds and feathers."

Gabrielle burst into tears and ran from the house as best she could in her awkward heels. She hated her cruel aunt, but knew in her heart that her aunt was right. Gabrielle never looked good or felt at ease in the extravagant dresses that were the style. She loved simple, comfortable clothes. What *was* she doing in this hideous dress? She couldn't wait for the night to end.

Gabrielle would later become famous as Coco Chanel and would make her simple style the very symbol of understated wealth and elegance. She would enter the elite world she always yearned to be a part of, and she would influence what the rich and famous wore. But she would never discuss her childhood.

Few of her upper-class friends and clients knew that the "Queen of Fashion" grew up as a peasant girl, in Auvergne, France. Her family was poor, and her mother died of tuberculosis when Gabrielle was a child. Her father, a traveling peddler, abandoned twelve-year-old Gabrielle and her two sisters at an orphanage, and they never saw him again.

Gabrielle's world was shattered, but she was too proud to show it. To the nuns at the orphanage, she was intelligent and a hard worker. As a teen, she had to choose between becoming a nun or continuing school; she chose school. But it wasn't easy. At the convent boarding school, wealthy students were kept separate from the charity cases like Gabrielle. She was humiliated by the distinction and decided to earn money for herself and her sisters by working as a seamstress.

For her school graduation, she worked night and day at a nearby aunt's house to design an original dress. Influenced by the romance novels she read and the fashion of the day, Gabrielle created the gaudy, layered gown of purple velvet that prompted her aunt's sharp comment. Never again would she stray from her own innate sense of style. Simple clothes in subtle colors would become her calling card.

After her graduation, she worked by day as a seamstress and by night as a *chanteuse*, or singer. It was in the Paris cabarets that she received her nickname "Coco." Although she didn't have the best voice, Coco's personality couldn't be ignored; she was one of the most popular singers in Paris. Soon she was being courted by wealthy, influential men and was introduced to Europe's high society.

Although she wanted to fit in with the counts and countesses and the dukes and

Coco got her name from a popular song she sang as a chanteuse, "Who Has Seen Coco?", about a lost dog!

duchesses, Coco was always a little different. The buxom women around her dressed in heavy layers of ruffles and fabrics and cinched their bodies tightly with girdles and corsets. Coco said of their outrageous hats, which weighed almost as much as they did, "How can the brain function in those things?"

Coco, a flat-chested tomboy who loved riding horses, knew she couldn't compete with these fashion butterflies, so she showed off her slim figure and beautiful neck with simple outfits she made herself, even borrowing pants, shirts and ties from her boyfriends. Her clothes were seen as radical, but her hats, at least, were a hit. Instead of huge concoctions of fruits, flowers and feathers, Coco designed smaller hats with a single feather, blossom or even nothing at all.

When she was twenty-five, a wealthy boyfriend, Guy Capel, loaned Coco the money to start her own store and design studio in a posh Paris neighborhood. At first her look was criticized as "severe." But with the first World War underway, even the wealthy women were working for the war effort. Out went the ornate dresses and hats and the elaborate underclothes. They were considered extravagant when men were suffering. In came simpler clothes—the jersey suit, the safari coat, and the "little black dress." Coco designed outfits for a freer woman. Practicality was the rule; women had to be able to move easily in her clothes. Soon she was "in." Wealthy women of Paris and all over Europe demanded all her latest creations. Even the critics changed their tune and pronounced her clothes "elegant."

Coco's fashions echoed her childhood with simple cuts, like her old school uniforms, and neutral colors, especially black, like the nuns' habits. These plain outfits were accented with ornate jewelry, like a church with its stained glass windows. She was also inspired by the clothes of the poor—a sailor's pants and cap, a schoolgirl's simple dress. Although they reflected her humble origins, Coco's clothes weren't cheap. After her years of poverty, she made sure her rich clients paid her well, and she knew that a high price tag would only

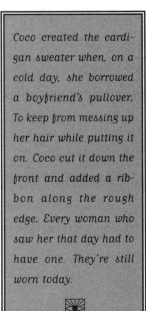

Coco created the cardigan sweater when, on a cold day, she borrowed a boyfriend's pullover. To keep from messing up her hair while putting it on, Coco cut it down the front and added a ribbon along the rough edge. Every woman who saw her that day had to have one. They're still worn today.

make her more in demand. As the 1920s approached, Coco set the standard for the "new woman"—slim and boyish, with bobbed, carefree hair, and financially independent. By the time she turned thirty, she was at the top of the fashion world.

She was also at the top of the social world. Always torn between creativity and financial security, wealthy Coco surrounded herself with artists. Pablo Picasso, Igor Stravinsky, and Salvador Dali all counted Coco as a friend.

With her designs in high demand, Coco soon paid back Guy Capel. But he married another woman soon afterward, since Coco's lower class background made her unsuitable for marriage in his eyes. Coco was devastated, but continued to see him even after the marriage. Their relationship ended when Guy died in a car crash. For the rest of her life, Coco dated many men but never married.

By the time she turned fifty, in 1933, her fashion empire employed nearly 4,000 workers and sold close to 28,000 designs each year! She also expanded into other areas of fashion. Her line of costume jewelry, which echoed the stained glass and church icons of her youth, was hugely successful. And when she set out to create a perfume, she knew it would have to be totally unique. Chanel No. 5 combined eighty flower essences, resulting in a fresh, youthful scent that lasted longer than other perfumes. Coco even made the bottle revolutionary. Instead of the romantic, curvy bottles most perfumes came in, Coco created a strong, square, androgynous bottle with only her name and a mysterious number. People were intrigued. Soon Chanel No. 5 was the most popular perfume in the world.

The very nature of fashion is that what's "in" today is "out" tomorrow. But Coco was never out for long. Her style is so timeless that she was the height of fashion at the turn of the century and in the 1930s, then again in the 1950s. Even in the

1980s, after her death, Coco's style rose from the grave. Today, her look is still the epitome of elegant, understated style.

A poor orphan, with no class or connections, Coco made herself into a millionaire and founded the very first fashion empire. She created the movement toward functional, comfortable, and practical clothing for women, which has been copied by the likes of Calvin Klein, Ralph Lauren, and Tommy Hilfiger. Coco was the original. She freed women from the weight of fashion, allowing them to look beautiful and stylish in clothing that let them lead active lifestyles. Coco's clothes were adored by women as different as Princess Grace, Marilyn Monroe, and Jackie Kennedy, and her timeless style has defined women's fashion for almost a century.

How Will You Rock the World?

"I have always loved fashion, a talent I got from my grandmas—one is a seamstress and the other does cross-stitch. I began making my own clothes years ago and now I model my outfits for American Cancer Society benefits. Someday I plan to have my own label and to work only with models who actually look like real people."

Jessica Sandine, age 14

"I will rock the world with my amazing artwork, making people smile when they see it. I plan to go to college on an art scholarship."

Desiree Golding, age 13

Eleanor Roosevelt

1884–1962 ⊕ *ActIvIst/UnIted NatIons Delegate* ⊕ *UnIted States*

You gain strength, courage, and confidence by every experience in which you really stop to look fear in the face . . . You must do the thing you think you cannot do.

— Eleanor Roosevelt

The little girl held tightly to Eleanor's hand as they walked through the dark slum. She was coughing and shivering in the cold night air.

"Will she be all right?" asked Franklin, wrapping her in his coat.

"I think so," answered Eleanor, her voice heavy with worry, "but we need to get her home and into bed."

Home, however, was not much better than the street. They took the girl to the dirty, overcrowded tenement room she shared with her large family. The ceiling was a sheet of tin, the floor a few rough planks, and the walls tar paper; the cold wind whistled through the many holes. They could see one stained mattress in the corner and a small table with no chairs. Otherwise the room was bare. A single candle lit the faces of the girl's parents and siblings. They looked hungry and tired.

Eleanor was used to seeing this kind of suffering; she'd been working with poor immigrant families for months. But Franklin was shocked. All the way home, he said again and again, "I can't believe human beings live that way." Nor could he believe that a girl of his social class was immersed in that world. But Eleanor wasn't like the other girls he knew.

Eleanor was just eighteen when she introduced Franklin Roosevelt—the man who would become her husband and, later, president of the United States—to a world he had never seen. She would serve to enlighten her husband and affect change upon the world for the rest of her life. As a teen she changed lives one at a time; later she would help people on a grand scale. Historians have called her "the most influential woman of our times" and many would argue that Eleanor did more to fight poverty, racism, sexism, and other injustices than any other woman in history. She was truly the "First Lady of the World."

The self-assurance Eleanor would be known for in later years was virtually non-existent during her childhood. Born to a well-known, upper class family, Eleanor was raised to be no more than a wealthy debutante and wife. For this job, a girl's main asset was beauty, not brains. Eleanor's mother was just such a beauty and worried over her daughter's looks. She often hurt the feelings of her serious, shy child by calling her "Granny." But when her mother got migraine headaches, she would let Eleanor rub her head for hours, and for the insecure girl, "the feeling that I was useful was perhaps the greatest joy I experienced." Eleanor's father, on the other hand, always let "his little Nell" know she was his favorite.

In spite of their wealth, the Roosevelts were not a happy family. Eleanor's parents fought bitterly about her father's drinking and affairs. Just when things looked like they couldn't get any worse, Eleanor's mother had her father committed to an asylum to get treatment for his alcoholism. Even after his release, he didn't come home, and Eleanor missed her father terribly. But tragedy really struck when Eleanor was eight. Her mother came down with diphtheria and died. The children saw their father briefly at the funeral, but then they were packed off to live with their grandmother, as their father was deemed unfit to raise them.

Grandmother Hall was a stern woman. Her house was a big, drafty, depressing place where noisy playing was forbidden, so Eleanor retreated even further into herself and books became her escape. Her only joy was visiting her father, but this was also stressful, as he grew more and more unpredictable. Once he took Eleanor to his private men's club in New York City and left her sitting out on the sidewalk. Six hours later, the doorman finally figured out who the girl was and told her Mr. Roosevelt had left hours before. She had to take a cab home. Two years after her mother's death, Eleanor's father died after taking a bad fall while drunk. Any happiness Eleanor had known disappeared. Her cousin remembered, "We were a gay ebullient family. Eleanor was just sad." This sadness would plague her for the rest of her life,

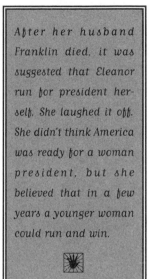

After her husband Franklin died, it was suggested that Eleanor run for president herself. She laughed it off. She didn't think America was ready for a woman president, but she believed that in a few years a younger woman could run and win.

but from her painful childhood sprang Eleanor's empathy and desire to help others who were suffering.

She finally escaped the dreariness of Grandmother Hall's when she was sent away to boarding school in England. Allenswood, a girls' school outside London, was run by a free-thinking French woman named Marie Souvestre. "Sou," as her students called her, believed that women should be more than ornaments; they should think for themselves and have their own opinions. She taught her girls not only about literature and art, but also about social and political issues.

Sou took a special interest in her shy American student. She brought Eleanor with her to Europe and encouraged her self-reliance by having the young girl make all their travel arrangements. Eleanor recalled these exciting times:

> *I felt that I was starting a new life, free from all my former sins and traditions . . . this was the first time in my life that my fears left me.*[11]

Eleanor learned, explored, debated and began to find herself. She was happy for the first time in her life.

Eleanor's happy freedom did not last long, however. Before she could start her senior year at Allenswood, Grandmother Hall called her back to America. Again, it was not her intellect that mattered. Eleanor was a debutante, after all, and at age eighteen it was time for her to make her official introduction to society. Although she was horrified, Eleanor had to obey. She returned to New York and began her rounds of parties and dances. Never good at small talk, Eleanor preferred to discuss serious issues, which was not considered "ladylike."

School, however, began a transformation in young Eleanor that could not be stopped. Despite the endless and meaningless social events on her calendar, she always found a way to bring meaning into her life. She volunteered in settlement houses—shelters for the thousands of immigrants flooding into New York at that time. Settlement houses were places they could go when they first arrived, penniless and scared. Working with poor families was a revelation for Eleanor. At Allenswood they had discussed poverty and injustice, but this was the first time she saw their reality. Unlike other high-society women, who just visited the settlement houses or donated money, Eleanor gave her time—and lots of it. She had always wanted to be useful, and now there were people who really needed her. She dove in.

Many of the families Eleanor worked with labored in sweatshops—factories that forced people to work long hours in terrible conditions for very small amounts of money. Eleanor began visiting these places and reporting her findings to the Consumers' League. She was terrified at first, but found strength in the anger these visits made her feel: "I saw little children of four or five sitting at tables until they dropped with fatigue."

During her social debut, Eleanor did meet one young man who was attracted to her ideas and opinions—handsome Franklin Delano Roosevelt, her fifth cousin, once removed. Franklin loved talking with her and thought she was the most fascinating woman he'd ever met. When he picked her up at the settlement houses, she opened his eyes to the world that existed outside their privileged cocoon. He'd never realized how much his fellow Americans were suffering, right under his nose. Franklin was deeply interested in the realities of life, and Eleanor showed him those realities. When he proposed, she was surprised, and asked why he would choose someone so plain. With her by his side, he answered, he might one day amount to something.

But after their marriage, Eleanor buried her newfound independence and social passion. Her domineering mother-in-law, her husband's career, and her constant pregnancies discouraged her from pursuing her own dreams. Over the next ten years, Eleanor gave birth to six children, five of whom survived.

As Franklin's political career took off, Eleanor's life improved. They moved away from his overbearing mother, and Eleanor began to emerge from her shell. With World War I, she got involved in her social causes again. She joined the Red Cross and cofounded the Navy Relief Fund, which served meals to hungry soldiers traveling through Washington, D.C. While inspecting hospitals for the Red Cross, she discovered the horrible living conditions and treatment of the mentally ill, many of whom had suffered breakdowns while fighting in the war. For the first time, Eleanor utilized her husband's political connections and was able to get increased funding to these institutions.

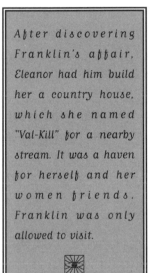

After discovering Franklin's affair, Eleanor had him build her a country house, which she named "Val-Kill" for a nearby stream. It was a haven for herself and her women friends. Franklin was only allowed to visit.

During this time of rebirth, Eleanor was dealt another catastrophe. She discovered Franklin was having an affair. For a woman whose childhood love had been uncertain, her husband's lie was crushing. "The bottom dropped out of my own particular world," she recalled. She had lived her life according to Franklin's needs for over a decade. Now she would have to stand on her own again. She offered Franklin a divorce, but he refused, partially because it would ruin his career, but also because he still cared about her. From then on, however, their marriage was more of a business partnership.

Eleanor dove back into politics. Women had recently won the right to vote, so she joined the League of Women Voters to help them make intelligent voting choices. She kept members up to date on issues like labor reform and children's rights, and helped edit the *Women's Democratic News*. She even worked for the Women's Trade Union League, a radical feminist group fighting to decrease the work week, to raise minimum wages, and to end child labor. When she and some friends took over the Todhunter School for Girls, Eleanor discovered another passion. As a teacher, she pushed and inspired her students as Sou had pushed and inspired her. When other duties began cutting into her school time, Eleanor was unhappy: "I teach because I love it. I cannot give it up."

In addition to her own interests, Eleanor continued to assist her husband and his career. In 1921, Franklin was diagnosed with polio, a paralyzing disease. He had difficulty walking for the rest of his life, relying on a cane, bulky leg braces, or a wheelchair. He also relied on his wife. Eleanor was often his legs. When Franklin was elected governor of New York in 1928, she began visiting state institutions he could not access, doing on-site inspections for him, reporting on what needed to be improved.

In 1929, the stock market crashed; banks and businesses failed, farmers lost their land, people lost their homes, and twelve million Americans lost their jobs. It was the start of the Great Depression. Franklin decided to run for president during this difficult time, promising to give the voters a "New Deal"—new relief programs, new jobs, new houses. Eleanor, however, was not excited about the idea of becoming First Lady. The wife of the President at that time was expected to host dinners, make small talk, and look good on her husband's arm, tasks Eleanor had hated since she was a teen. And she dreaded giving up her political and social work. But when Franklin won in 1932, Eleanor made the most of her new role.

Just as young Eleanor was unlike any girl Franklin had ever met, Eleanor, wife of the president, was unlike any First Lady the nation had ever seen. As one Maine lobsterman put it, "She ain't stuck up, she ain't dressed up, and she ain't afeared to talk." Franklin held press conferences, and so did Eleanor. That was a first. And to encourage newspapers to employ more women, she only allowed female reporters into her popular press conferences. She felt struggling Americans needed some encouraging contact from the White House, so Eleanor began giving radio talks, writing monthly magazine articles, and later writing a popular daily newspaper column called "My Day." She asked citizens to write her about their problems, their hopes and their dreams. She received over 300,000 letters in one year.

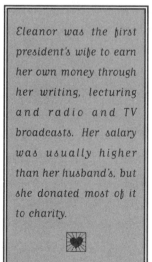

Eleanor was the first president's wife to earn her own money through her writing, lecturing and radio and TV broadcasts. Her salary was usually higher than her husband's, but she donated most of it to charity.

She did not give up her political work either, but now played a more powerful role from behind the scenes. As always, she had a considerable influence on her husband, convincing him to put women into top government posts.

She traveled the country, reporting back to him on how Americans were surviving the Depression and whether government programs were helping. Eleanor brought comfort and reassurance to the communities she visited, becoming a champion of the poor.

Eleanor also fought racism. She invited black political leaders, as well as poor farmers, to the White House to discuss issues, and she supported the National Association for the Advancement of Colored People (NAACP) in their fight for equal rights, as well as a controversial federal law against lynching (the beating and hanging to death of blacks without trial and often without any reason besides racial hatred). She was harshly criticized for her beliefs, and not even Franklin had the courage to pass the anti-lynching law (he needed the support of racist politicians for the New Deal programs). Politician Adlai Stevenson applauded her courage:

> Long before the civil rights issue moved to the forefront of the
> nation's consciousness, she was there, earning public abuse for her
> quiet reminders of the inequalities practiced in our land.[12]

In 1939, the strength of her convictions was really put to the test. Eleanor belonged to a prestigious group called Daughters of the American Revolution (DAR); members were women from old, important American families, like the Roosevelts. When the DAR refused to let Marian Anderson, a world-famous singer and friend of Eleanor's, perform at DAR's Constitution Hall because she was black, Eleanor was outraged, and took a very public stand.

She announced her resignation from the DAR and condemned their racism. Her action drew worldwide attention to the cause and got all of America talking about equal rights. She then helped arrange for Marian to sing a free concert at the Lincoln Memorial. In front of an enormous statue of the president who freed the slaves, Marian gave an electrifying performance to a crowd of 75,000 people. As she sang the spiritual "Nobody Knows the Trouble I've Seen," the audience was moved to tears.

But the trouble brewing in America was eclipsed by the war exploding in Europe. By 1939, World War II was under way, and, a year later, Franklin was elected to an unprecedented third term as president (presidents now can only serve two terms). Although Eleanor was generally a pacifist, she believed that America had to stop Hitler's quest for world domination and extermination of the Jews. She took on her first official government position when she became the director of the Office of Civil Defense.

At fifty-nine, Eleanor traveled to the war front in the South Pacific to check on the troops and boost morale. At first, Admiral William "Bull" Halsey was against her visit, thinking a woman on the battlefield would be a nuisance. Eleanor proved him wrong by conducting a thorough inspection of the hospitals and visiting each wounded soldier, asking his name, if he needed anything, and could she take a message home for him. Admiral Halsey changed his tune, saying, "She alone had accomplished more good than any other person, or any group of civilians, who had passed through my area." Eleanor worked so hard—traveling 23,000 miles, visiting seventeen islands and 400,000 men—that she lost thirty pounds!

> During her trip to the South Pacific, Eleanor visited the indigenous people of New Zealand, the Maoris. They were so taken with the friendly First Lady, they named her "Kotoku," or "white heron of one flight," after a magical creature from their legends that is seen just once in a lifetime.

Franklin held out just long enough to make sure America and its allies won the war. After he died in 1945, most people expected Eleanor to pack her bags and retire from public life. Instead, she began working for world peace. Since the end of World War I, she'd been advocating for an international peace-keeping organization. In 1945, her dream came true when the United Nations (U.N.) was formed, and President Truman asked her to be a delegate. During her seven years with the U.N., Eleanor was the only woman to represent the U.S. When she started, other members doubted her abilities. She quickly changed their minds, working to create and fight for a Universal Declaration of Human Rights. When it was finally passed, the delegates gave Eleanor a standing ovation.

As she entered her seventies, Eleanor never slowed down. After the war and her work in the U.N., she passionately believed that America needed to stay involved in the world, not retreat. Realizing her diplomatic expertise, Truman sent her to India, Pakistan, and the Middle East to

> When Truman was sworn in after FDR's death, he asked Eleanor if there was anything he could do for her. She replied, "Is there anything I can do for you? For you are the one in trouble now."

build relationships for the U.S. And in 1961, Eleanor was again appointed as a delegate to the U.N. by newly-elected President John Kennedy. When she returned to her old job, she was greeted by her second standing ovation!

At a time in life when most women would be sewing quilts or relaxing in a rocking chair, Eleanor stayed active, both physically and mentally. "I could not, at any age," she said, "be content to take my place in a corner by the fireside and simply look on. Life was meant to be lived." She continued to live her life—working as a professor at Brandeis University, lobbying for the Equal Rights Amendment, and campaigning for her favorite candidates—until her very last day. In 1962, just after her seventy-eighth birthday, she died of tuberculosis, and the world lost one of its greatest heroines.

When Eleanor's Universal Declaration of Human Rights was finally adopted by the U.N. after years of hard work, she was so elated that the 64-year-old took a running slide down the U.N.'s marble hallway!

Eleanor devoted her life to improving the world, first, as a young woman, volunteering for those who needed her help; then, as First Lady, advising her husband and responding to the needs of America; and, finally, on her own, as a delegate to the United Nations. She entered politics because of her husband, but remained because of her own beliefs and passions. Even when her outspoken opinions on controversial issues—women voting and civil rights—got her in trouble, Eleanor refused to back down. She stood up for what she believed in, what she thought was right. This courage and strength of character made her one of the most admired, respected, and powerful women in the world.

If anyone were to ask me what I want out of life I would say—the opportunity for doing something useful, for in no other way, I am convinced, can true happiness be attained.

— Eleanor Roosevelt

How Will You Rock the World?

"So far there have only been men presidents, so I will rock the world by becoming the first girl president."

Kaitlyn Midori Shepardson, age 11

"I'm going to run for city council because I have so many ideas about improving my hometown. If I prove myself worthy, I will run for governor, and later for president. When my term is up, I will be an ambassador to Germany or Sweden. Or I might join the Peace Corps. I am going to seriously fight to make a difference in my world."

Jessica Turner-Whitmore, age 12

"I want to rock the world by giving money to the people who need it, because I think that poverty is big problem striking the world today. I will also rock the world by showing the value of love to everyone—people need love to encourage them and help them succeed!"

Kendra Emana Jackson, age 10

Mary Pickford

1893–1979 ❀ ACTRESS/PRODUCER ❀ CANADA/UNITED STATES

*The best known woman
who has ever lived, the
woman who was known
to more people and
loved by more people
than any other woman
that has been in
all history.*

— journalist Adela Rogers
St. Johns, praising Mary
in 1980

The tiny girl with blond curls and dark eyes could see her mother crying in the kitchen. Ever since her father died, Gladys had seen her mother cry a lot. She knew it was because she was sad and lonely, but also because she worried about how she would take care of Gladys and the other children. She tiptoed into the kitchen, took her mother's hands in her own, and gazed up into her eyes.

"Mama, have you next month's rent and money for coal?"

"No, darling," she whispered to her young daughter, "but don't worry, we'll get it somehow."

"Tell me again how old I must be before I can earn money for us?"

Gladys' mother lifted her daughter's hands and uncurled each pudgy finger until all ten were outstretched—ten years old. Gladys already took care of her younger siblings and helped her mother clean and cook, but she was thrilled to know that, in just five years, she could help the family even more. Then maybe her mother would stop crying and they could be happy again.

Gladys Louise Smith (who later changed her name to Mary Pickford) would begin to help her struggling family even sooner than she expected. At eight, she would launch her acting career and become the breadwinner for the Smith clan. Her desire to help her family and to make her mother happy would always fuel Gladys's ambitions, and, indeed, one day she would lift her entire family out of poverty forever and become one of the richest, most beloved and powerful women in the world.

Gladys was born in Toronto, Canada, in 1893. Her father, John, was a handsome and charming alcoholic who couldn't hold down a job. Even when he did work, the family was poor and Gladys's mother, Charlotte, took in extra sewing to make ends meet. It came as a shock to them all when John died—he had abandoned the family while searching for work. Life got even tougher. Charlotte had three children to feed, so she sewed full time and rented rooms in the house to boarders, but it wasn't enough. She was certain that she'd have to break up the family and send the children to better homes. Indeed, many wealthy Toronto couples were eager to take in the adorable Smith siblings.

But young Gladys wouldn't have any of it:

> *A determination was born in me . . . that nothing could crush:*
> *I must try to take my father's place . . . and prevent anything from*
> *breaking up my family.*[13]

Although her mother made her promise not to work until she was ten, Gladys jumped at her chance when a boarder suggested she try out for a play. The eight-year-old girl begged her reluctant mother to let her try. Charlotte had reason to worry about this type of work; the theater at the turn of the last century was considered a "den of evil." It was certainly not a wholesome place for children or "ladies," like Charlotte. But when Gladys and her siblings won paying roles in a play, their mother gave in for the sake of keeping the family together. Gladys was paid eight dollars a week. She gave every penny to her mother.

As a girl, Mary ate roses, hoping to ingest their beauty.

All the Smith children performed, but it was Gladys who really shone. She loved the stage, calling it "my playhouse . . . my nursery . . . my school." Soon she was winning all the starring child roles and was dubbed "Baby Gladys" by an adoring public. By age ten, she and the family began traveling all over

Canada and the United States, performing in touring shows. At first the family was excited, but the thrill soon wore off. They slept most nights sitting up on trains, and what hotels they could afford were seedy and dangerous. They never stayed in one place for more than a few days, usually boarding a train immediately after the curtain fell. For five years, Gladys grew up with no friends, no house, no school, no pets—no life. She and her family were miserable.

> *Mary went to school for just three months in her life. She learned to read off the billboards she saw while traveling with the theater.*

By the time Gladys was fifteen, she knew she was ready for something better. She was desperate to work for David Belasco, a famous Broadway producer, but when he refused to give her an audition or even meet with her, she stormed into his partner's office and told him, "My life depends on seeing Mr. Belasco!" It worked. Belasco was so amused that he gave her an audition and then a role in his next play. He also renamed her Mary Pickford.

Broadway theater was a step up—the pay was higher, the dressing rooms better, and Mary and her family got to stay put for a while—but still, she never knew when she might stop getting work. Although she soon became a Broadway star—her childhood dream—she still worried about financial security.

To supplement the off-and-on theater money, Charlotte suggested Mary work in the "flickers." Flickers were a brand new technology, the earliest form of silent movies. If theater was considered a shady occupation, flickers were worse. They were

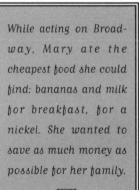

> *While acting on Broadway, Mary ate the cheapest food she could find: bananas and milk for breakfast, for a nickel. She wanted to save as much money as possible for her family.*

the entertainment of the lower class, who couldn't afford theater tickets. Shows cost just a nickel and played in seedy storefronts called "nickelodeons." Mary didn't want to tarnish her good name—she considered flickers "cheap," "loathsome," and "a complete disgrace"—but she did it for her mother. After all, flickers paid five dollars per day and offered plenty of work.

She got her start in movies at Biograph Studio, acting for the soon-to-be-legendary director D.W. Griffith. He would go down in history as the man who invented movies as we know them today—in great part thanks to Mary's starring in his pictures. Sixteen-year-old Mary was such a natural on the screen, she was promoted to leading lady after just one movie. With her curly golden locks and her huge, haunting eyes, Mary dazzled audiences. They dubbed her "Goldilocks" and "The Biograph Girl." And unlike the theater, there was never a lack of work. That first year, Mary made forty-five movies!

Although Mary had almost no formal education, she was always sharp when it came to business. She *had* to be—her family's security depended on it. She refused to be a "nice lady" and leave the room while the "studio boys" made the deals. Mary knew just what kind of deals she wanted, and she got them. One producer griped, "It often took longer to make one of Mary's contracts than it did to make one of Mary's pictures."

At the start of her movie career, she demanded and received almost double the pay of the other actors, before D.W. Griffith even saw her act! Later, she made producers compete for her. She would work only for whoever paid the most and gave her creative control. "I had to assume the business role in order to protect the thing I loved, my work," she explained. And when she was criticized for her "unladylike" business tactics, she replied, "I don't think the brain has any sex."

Mary and director D.W. Griffith both had strong personalities and fought often. Once Mary was so offended by his insults, she actually bit him!

When she moved on to Zukor's Famous Players Company, Mary was paid $500 per week at a time when most factory workers, teachers and farmers earned $500 or less in a year! Mary began shooting films in California, where Hollywood was still a wild, hilly wilderness, full of coyotes and cactus, outside of Los Angeles. It was there she met the top actors of the time, including the dashing Douglas Fairbanks and his best friend Charlie Chaplin. Mary became a star playing street-smart heroines in *Tess of the Storm Country* (1914), *Pollyanna* (1920), *Rebecca of Sunnybrook Farm* (1917) and *Poor Little Rich Girl* (1917), and was nicknamed "America's Sweetheart" by her millions of fans.

Mary fell in love with her handsome friend Douglas, while they were both still married to others. When they divorced their spouses and married each other, it was the scandal of the century, but their fans quickly forgave them, and they soon were the first "power couple" of Hollywood. A common occurrence for actors today, Mary and Douglas were the first stars to be mobbed by adoring fans when they went out in public. The mansion they built, Pickfair (a combination of their names), became the social mecca of Hollywood. Their parties were world-famous, attracting guests like Charlie Chaplin and even Albert Einstein.

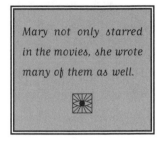

Mary not only starred in the movies, she wrote many of them as well.

When America got involved in World War I, the U.S. government recruited the biggest stars—Pickford, Fairbanks, and Chaplin—to tour the country selling bonds to raise money for the war effort. Mary devoted herself to the cause. She cut her hair and auctioned her precious curls, her photographs decorated the trenches, the Navy named her their "Little Sister," and when people gave to the Red Cross, she autographed their receipts. The war experience had a huge effect on Mary's conscience. Not only did she keep supporting her family, but she used her wealth to help soldiers and veterans by setting up educational scholarships. Remembering her own days of hunger and struggle, she also founded the Motion Picture Relief Fund to give aid to out-of-work actors.

In 1919, at a time when most women didn't even work outside the home, Mary, along with Douglas, Charlie, William Hart, and D.W. Griffith (called "the Big Five" at the time), formed their own production company, United Artists. Once again, this was a shrewd business move, as it gave the actors total control in selecting which movies they would make, how those movies were sold to theaters, and how much money they could earn. Theirs was the first production company ever started and run by the artists themselves. It was a novel concept. Before United Artists, studios saw actors as merchandise to be bought and sold, not as people with valuable opinions. One producer summed up Hollywood's reaction to actors running their own studios: "The lunatics have taken over the asylum!"

At United Artists, Mary produced numerous movies each year; selecting, co-writing, acting in, and making the business decisions for each one. Her marriage to Fairbanks soured, and everyone else in her family died between 1928 and 1939. Mary was exhausted from the emotional turmoil. When "talkies" (the first movies with sound) made their debut, she knew her days were numbered, so, in 1933 she retired. Mary won her first Academy Award in 1929 for *Coquette*; she won her last in 1976 for her lifetime achievements in film. That was her final public appearance. She died of a brain hemorrhage in 1979, at age eighty-six.

Mary was the original "movie star," acting in some of the first films ever made and helping make the new art form as popular as it is today. While her fans called her "Little Mary," she was always a strong and intelligent person—she didn't become a millionaire just because of her sweet face. She earned mountains more than most other actors of her time because she paid attention to how the business worked and demanded her fair share. The studio she helped create, United Artists, is still producing films today. Mary set the stage for actors who not only wanted to be stars, but also wanted to have some say over their futures.

How Will You Rock the World?

"I want to be a film-maker because of the strong voice it would give me in society. 'Grace,' they tell me, 'You're just one person; you can't change the world!' Well, I've got

news for them. One person <u>can</u> change the world. It could be me. It could be you. All we have to do is stop looking at the <u>can'ts</u> and the <u>impossibles</u> and realize what we're made of."

Grace Marek, age 13

"I will rock the world by winning a Tony Award in a Broadway play. I'm already performing

in the Children's Educational Theatre, which is hard to get into."

Samantha Rosen, age 10

Golda Meir

1898–1978 🖋 *PRIME MINISTER* 🖋 *ISRAEL*

There is only one thing I hope to see before I die, and that is that my people should not need expressions of sympathy anymore.
— Golda Meir

"**N**o daughter of mine is going to stand on a box in the street and make a spectacle of herself. It is a *shandeh* (a disgrace)!" shouted Golda's father, his face red with fury. Seventeen-year-old Golda tried to explain that she had already promised herself and her friends that she would give the speech in front of the synagogue. She tried to explain that her past speeches had been very successful at getting the neighborhood Jews excited about helping their comrades in far-off Palestine. But her angry father didn't hear a word she said as he yelled, "If you go, I will follow you and pull you home by your braid!" Golda went anyway, but she could feel her body shaking as she climbed atop her box to speak to the large crowd.

She spoke passionately about the brave Jews in Palestine, men *and* women, who were struggling to create a nation where all Jews around the world would be welcome and safe from persecution. Thankfully, she couldn't see her father in the crowd, but she could see the eyes of her audience lighting up with pride and determination. At the end of her speech there was a long roar of applause and even more people volunteering to help the cause. Golda wondered if maybe her father hadn't come after all. When she returned home to face her father's punishment, her mother met her at the door. "Your father is asleep now," she said, "but he did hear you speak. He was amazed. He said to me, 'I don't know where she gets it from.'" Golda's father was so moved by her words that he forgot his threat entirely. Golda considered it the most successful speech she ever made.

Golda Mabovitch, born in 1898, spent the first five years of her life in Kiev, Russia. Even at such a young age, Golda experienced the struggles of the Jewish people of Europe. Mobs of angry Russians often destroyed the homes and shops of their Jewish neighbors, sometimes even beating and killing them, but Russian police did nothing to help the Jews. When the Jewish community protested the brutality by holding a one-day fast, five-year-old Golda insisted on fasting, too, against her family's wishes.

It didn't take long for Golda's father to realize that it was getting too dangerous to be Jewish and live in Russia. He decided to move his family to the United States. After a long and dangerous journey, eight-year-old Golda and her family arrived in America and settled in Milwaukee, Wisconsin. At first Golda was overwhelmed by all the extravagances of America—running water, electric lights, trolleys, flushing toilets—but soon she happily settled into the large community of Russian Jews in her neighborhood. Her mother set up a general store below their apartment and Golda opened it in the mornings while her mother bought supplies at the market.

Because she worked mornings in the shop, Golda was often late for school. A policeman lectured Golda's mother about truancy, but since she spoke little English, she didn't understand him. Golda continued being late.

Golda loved school and was a good student. At age eleven, she began the public speaking and fundraising that would make her so famous later in life. When she realized that many of her classmates couldn't afford to buy their own schoolbooks, Golda recruited a group of girls to raise money. They called themselves the American Young Sisters Society and organized a "ball" which attracted dozens of people. They served food and read poetry, and Golda gave a speech. The event was so successful that they raised enough money to buy books for all the poor children of the school.

During Golda's childhood, most people didn't go to high school, especially not girls. Most girls went to work or got married as teens. When Golda told her parents that she planned to go to high school and then to college, they began secret negotiations to marry her off to a man twice her age! Golda found out and ran away to live with her older sister in Denver, Colorado.

In Denver, she not only went to high school, but also got involved in the growing Zionist movement. The Zionists believed that the Jewish people should create a new nation in their ancient homeland. Thousands of years ago, the Jewish religion was founded in the deserts of the Middle East (which they called Zion), where the Jews lived peacefully until the Romans drove them out and renamed the area Palestine. The Jews spread out around the world, mostly in countries that didn't want them, and many longed to return to Zion. Golda was inspired by what she heard of the Jewish pioneers in Palestine who were working to reclaim the desert and create a Jewish nation. To support their efforts, Golda spent hours on the streets of Denver raising money for Jewish pioneers to buy Palestinian land from the Turkish and Arab landowners.

Golda returned home, entered a teacher's college, and became even more active in the Zionist movement. Although she was too young, members of the Labor Zionist Party were so impressed with Golda's work that they accepted her into the party at age seventeen. In 1917, nineteen-year-old Golda decided it was time to go to Palestine herself to help build the Jewish nation she'd been dreaming of all her life. Just before she left, she married Morris Meyerson, a man she'd fallen in love with back in Denver. They left for Palestine together.

Golda and Morris moved onto a kibbutz (a community of people living and working together toward common goals). The group raised all their own food, built communal housing, and shared everything—money, clothes, even children! Kibbutzes across Palestine were working to transform "unusable" desert

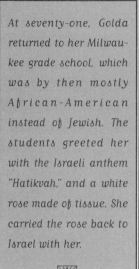

At seventy-one, Golda returned to her Milwaukee grade school, which was by then mostly African-American instead of Jewish. The students greeted her with the Israeli anthem "Hatikvah," and a white rose made of tissue. She carried the rose back to Israel with her.

into productive farms so that Jews could have a place to live that would sustain them. Golda loved the work and was good at making improvements. She was soon elected to make decisions for her kibbutz and to help decide the future of other Jewish settlements in Palestine. Golda had never been happier.

She and her husband took a break from the kibbutz to start a family and Golda gave birth to a son and then a daughter. Although she loved her children, Golda missed her work. After four years of domestic life, Golda decided to return to creating a nation for the Jews. She was a passionate, hard worker, and soon became a leader of the growing nation.

In the 1930s, just as Golda's political life began taking off, life for Jews in Europe deteriorated rapidly. All over Europe, they were being persecuted more strongly than before, and, in Germany, Hitler and his Nazis began attacking the Jews. Seventy thousand refugees fled to Palestine, their only safe haven. The Arabs of Palestine, however, strongly opposed increased Jewish immigration. They attacked Jewish settlements and demanded the British government (the colonial power in the area) stop letting in refugees. In 1939, just as Hitler was forcing European Jews into his deadly concentration camps, the British put the brakes on immigration and outlawed the purchase of Arab land. The Zionists were enraged. They knew their European family and friends would die if they couldn't get to Israel. They felt they had no choice but to fight.

During Hitler's reign, successful Jewish doctors, teachers, lawyers and businessmen fled to Israel to start over as farmers and laborers.

Golda joined *Haganah*, the Jewish secret underground army, which began smuggling as many Jewish refugees as possible into Palestine. Boats were built in secret and sent to rescue European Jews. Upon returning, the boats had to sneak past the British blockade of ships and unload the refugees in the dark of night. Back on shore, also under a cloak of darkness, members of the Haganah would carry pre-built housing to a new village site. When the sun came up, there would be a new town full of rescued immigrants! Her increased workload and worry over saving European Jews put a strain on Golda's marriage, and, in 1941, she and her husband separated.

From 1945-1950, half a million Jewish refugees flooded Israel!

In 1946, after World War II ended, England decided to let the Jews create their nation, but Golda and her government knew that when the British pulled out, surrounding Arab countries would move in and attack. Golda went to the U.S. to raise money for arms to protect the future nation. In a fundraising speech in Chicago, Golda said proudly to the Jewish crowd, "You cannot decide whether we will fight or not. We will . . . Whether we live or not, this is a decision you have to make." Her speeches were so effective that she returned with $50 million for the army. Her fellow politicians were astounded at the fortune Golda raised and credited her with saving the country from a certain doom.

> Golda endangered her own life trying to build peace with the opposition. She disguised herself as an Arab woman and traveled through enemy territory to meet with the leader of a neighboring Arab country. Sadly, her courageous bid for peace was unsuccessful.

In 1948, the U.N. took a vote, and the Jewish nation of Israel was born. Israel's leaders were elated and signed a proclamation of independence, outlining the goals of their new nation. As Golda signed her name, she wept uncontrollably. When someone asked why she was crying, Golda replied, "Because it breaks my heart to think of all those who should been here today and are not."

Fighting between the Jews and the Arabs began almost immediately. Thanks to Golda's fundraising, Israel was able to defend itself from all attacks. In a rush of national pride, Golda changed her name from Meyerson to the

> In Moscow, Golda was greeted by over 50,000 Russian Jews, who came to meet her and celebrate the founding of Israel. They were defying their oppressive government, and their courage affected Golda deeply.

Hebrew Meir and began work in the new government, first as Israel's ambassador to Russia, then as minister of labor. When she became foreign minister, Israel responded to threats from Egypt by capturing their territory—the Sinai Peninsula and the Gaza Strip. Explaining Israel's attack to the United Nations, she said, "We desire nothing more than peace, but we cannot equate peace merely with an apathetic readiness to be destroyed." And again in 1967, when the countries around Israel joined together in a plan to "push the Jews into the sea," the Jews launched a surprise attack and won a complete victory.

After forty years of hard work establishing a country for the Jews, Golda was ready to retire. Israel, however, wasn't ready to let her go. When the prime minister died in 1969, Golda was asked to replace him. At age seventy-one, Golda became the leader of the Jewish nation she dreamed of as a teen. During her five years as prime minister, Golda exhausted herself building the country up and defending it from enemy countries outside and terrorists inside its borders. Even after resigning from her post, she continued to work for peace, meeting with Egypt's president Anwar Sadat in 1977.

In 1978, Golda's strength finally gave out, and she died of the cancer she had been secretly battling for fifteen years. To the people of Israel, Golda will always be a symbol of their nation's birth, and will be remembered for guiding the country through its most challenging and exciting period in history. The rest of us will remain in awe of her progression from a young girl fundraising for her poorer classmates to the prime minister of Israel.

The miracle of Golda Meir was how one person could perfectly embody the spirit of so many.

— The New York Times

How Will You Rock the World?

"I would rock the world by putting an end to negative stereotypes. Stereotypes have led to many wars because people develop negative thoughts about each other. Once you think negatively about someone, your whole mind is set on that idea—just by  looking at a person you judge them, sometimes just from what you've heard, without knowing the real truth. I will fight stereotypes through my writing, by keeping my mind open and by respecting those who dare to be different."

Alina Din, age 14

Marian Anderson

1897–1993 ✤ *SINGER* ✤ *UNITED STATES*

A voice like yours is heard just once in a hundred years.
— famous conductor Arturo Toscanini, complimenting Marian

G iuseppe Boghetti barely looked up when the teenage girl walked in. He frowned and continued scribbling notes onto his sheet music.

"You know," he barked, "I'm seeing you just as a favor to your principal."

Marian could feel her body trembling. Could she really bring herself to sing for this man? Mr. Boghetti was one of the most respected voice coaches in the country. Why should he listen to her?

"I don't want any new students. I have too many already." Her heart sank some more, but he waved his hand at her to begin singing.

To calm her nerves, she closed her eyes and tried to forget where she was and who she was singing for. As she sang her favorite spiritual, "Deep River," Marian's rich, powerful voice poured out over the room, "Deep river, my home is over Jordan. . . ."

She finished and opened her eyes. The room was silent. Mr. Boghetti had his eyes closed, too, and seemed to be frozen, holding his breath. "Oh no, he hated it!" Marian thought in a panic.

After an eternity, the gruff teacher opened his eyes and looked at Marian for a long time.

"I will make room for you right away," he said. She clamped her hands over her mouth so she wouldn't scream from happiness.

"I will need only two years with you. After that you will be able to go any-where and sing for anybody."

Marian was overjoyed, but now she had a different worry. She wondered if the money her church had raised for her music lessons would be enough. Mr. Boghetti's fees would not be cheap. But when she asked him about it, he surprised her again. He said he would waive his regular fees; he would teach Marian for free. She couldn't believe her luck! Finally, her dreams were coming true. Maybe she really would be a famous concert singer.

Marian was born in 1897 in Philadelphia, Pennsylvania. Her father worked hard delivering ice and coal, and made enough money so her mother could stay home and take care of the children. Marian grew up in a happy family, surrounded by lots of love. From a very early age, she loved music, but her parents couldn't afford to buy instruments or lessons. So Marian made her own music. At age three, she began to sing.

By the time she was six, she was the star of her church choir. Her voice was deep and rich; she was what musicians call a *contralto*, the lowest female voice, but she could sing higher notes and lower notes as well. In fact, when her choir learned a song, Marian taught herself *all* the parts, high and low, so if a singer missed a performance, Marian could fill in.

Her family's life became much more difficult when Marian turned twelve, and her father died in a work accident. Her mother had to clean peo-ple's houses to support the family, and, though she never complained, she worked nonstop to keep her children fed and clothed. Marian desperately wanted to help. Although she dreamed of being a singer, she began training for more practi-

> *Marian never had problems projecting her voice. As a girl, her mother told her to imagine the black people who were only given seats way back in the balconies. She always made sure those back seats could hear her voice too.*

cal work. She learned to type so she could become a secretary and help support the family when she finished high school.

Her voice, however, was so amazing that, throughout high school, people hired her to sing at church gatherings, parties and club meetings, paying her $5 for each performance. This was a lot of money to Marian; she began to think that maybe she wouldn't have to become a secretary after all. But she knew that to be a professional singer, she would need professional training.

She decided to apply for lessons at a local music school, but they turned her away with a harsh rejection: "We don't take colored." Marian was crushed. She knew racism existed, but she had grown up in a neighborhood where whites and blacks respected each other. This was the first time Marian experienced racism *personally*, and she was horrified. She was ready to give up her singing dreams right then and there. "The way that woman spoke, it bit into my soul," she told her mother. "You must have faith," was the answer her mother gave back. "There will be another way for you to learn what you need to know."

And there *was* another way. Marian's church believed in her dreams, so when the members heard about her troubles, they raised money for private lessons. That's how she came to audition for Giuseppe Boghetti. That year she graduated from high school and began to sing professionally all over Pennsylvania at churches, colleges, and small theaters. Her fee went up to $100 per show! It was the happiest day in Marian's life when she told her mother, "I can take care of you now. You don't have to work anymore."

In 1925, Marian got her big break. She entered a singing contest with 300 competitors. First prize was a concert in New York City with the New York Philharmonic Orchestra. Marian surprised many, including herself, when she won. Her performance with the famous orchestra was a success, and Marian had every reason to believe her career was underway and that invitations to sing in America's best concert halls would pour in.

She was mistaken. Although the Civil War had freed the slaves almost sixty years before, America was still a very segregated and racist place. "Jim Crow" laws (named for an obedient black character in a minstrel show) barred blacks from sitting in the same seats as whites on buses or trains, eating in the same restaurants, or even performing on the same stages. Signs all over America read "Whites Only." Marian wasn't invited to sing in America's best concert halls because she was black, and even when she could sing, many white ticket buyers didn't believe a black woman could have any talent.

With her career at a standstill, Marian decided her only option was Europe. She left in 1930 and toured there for the next five years. Although she was still unknown in America, she was accepted as a great singer in Europe and even sang for the kings and queens of Sweden, Norway, Denmark, and England. Marian was very happy abroad, not just with her success, but because the weight of racism was lifted from her shoulders. She could sit in any seat, stay at any hotel, eat at any restaurant, perform anywhere she wanted, and earn a living as a singer. Europeans didn't care about her skin color, just her voice. But she missed her family and home. She dreamed of returning to America and making it a better place to live and perform.

Sitting in the audience of a Paris concert hall one night was Sol Hurok, manager of some of the world's greatest stars (he helped launch Anna Pavlova's career, among others). After the show, he asked to represent Marian on her return to America. It was another dream come true. Fellow show biz experts warned Hurok that America still wasn't ready. "You won't be able to *give* her away," they predicted. Not much had changed in five years.

But with Sol's help, Marian made a triumphant return to America in 1935 with a concert in New York's famous Town Hall. The audience gave her a standing ovation and the critics raved, "Marian Anderson has returned to her native land one of the great singers of our time." She was home.

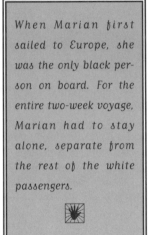

When Marian first sailed to Europe, she was the only black person on board. For the entire two-week voyage, Marian had to stay alone, separate from the rest of the white passengers.

In 1939, after singing in most European capitals, Marian tried to arrange a concert in Washington D.C. The theater, Constitution Hall, was owned by the Daughters of the American Revolution (DAR), a group of women whose families had, years ago, fought for America's freedom from England. Ironically, these women, descendants of men who fought for freedom, refused to let Marian sing on their stage. It was for "white artists only." First Lady Eleanor Roosevelt, herself a DAR member, resigned from the group in protest. This event sparked one of the first great civil rights debates of the twentieth century. Americans of both colors argued openly about the rights of blacks and waited to see what would happen.

What happened was a quiet revolution. Marian was invited, instead, to sing a free concert in front of the Lincoln Memorial. It was a symbolic location for the event, at the foot of a statue of the man who drafted the Emancipation Proclamation, freeing the slaves. The concert drew an unbelievable 75,000 fans (and millions more on radio). Marian was so astonished by the show of support that, afterwards, she remembered nothing of her time on stage. The audience, however, would never forget it.

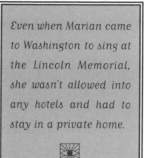

Even when Marian came to Washington to sing at the Lincoln Memorial, she wasn't allowed into any hotels and had to stay in a private home.

She opened with "America," and one observer recalled blacks and whites in the audience singing along with Marian, "Our country 'tis of thee, sweet land of li-ber-ty, of thee I sing . . ."

> *She put such great emphasis upon liberty. The DAR's refusal to allow her to sing was a breach of that liberty. There were tears in my eyes. I think there were tears in the eyes of almost everybody in that huge crowd.*[14]

When she finished with ". . . let freedom ring," America was listening. One journalist applauded Marian's courage: "That concert struck at the very depths of racism in America." Years before Martin Luther King, Jr. would stand in the same spot and deliver his "I Have a Dream" speech, Marian Anderson pricked the nation's conscience with her own dreams of equality.

She continued breaking through the color barrier for the rest of her career. She performed at the White House and at presidential inaugurations; she sang in Russia, Israel, and Japan, and, during World War II, she finally appeared at Constitution Hall. In 1955 she achieved yet another of her goals; she became the first black person to perform at the world-famous Metropolitan Opera in New York City. Again, the audience showed its support for Marian's efforts in changing America. They gave her a standing ovation even *before* she began singing her part.

Her every childhood dream realized, Marian kept on singing. In 1957, the State Department sent her on a twelve-nation tour as a goodwill ambassador for America. A year later they made it official and appointed Marian as a delegate to the United Nations. Marian didn't retire from singing until she was almost seventy years old, giving a farewell tour of the U.S. in 1964-65. During her career, she was honored with countless awards, including the 1939 Spingarn Medal, given to the Black American who achieved the most, and the 1963

Presidential Medal of Freedom, the highest award a president can give a citizen during peacetime.

Many people believe that because of Marian's pure voice and tremendous range, she was the world's greatest contralto. But her impact was not limited to her voice. Her obituary summed up Marian's lasting memory: "[She] maintained a quiet dignity while transcending the racial and cultural barriers imposed on her artistry." She showed Americans—black and white—what blacks could do if given the chance. Her success opened music to all the black artists who followed her—Stevie Wonder, Diana Ross, Michael Jackson, and even Mariah Carey—and made it one of the first fields

Orpheus Fisher first asked Marian to marry him just after high school. She said no because she knew it would interfere with her career. Fisher waited twenty years, until Marian had achieved her dreams, before she said yes.

in which black Americans could achieve greatness and be recognized for their talents. Her courage and insistence on the right of all Americans to pursue their dreams also paved the way for future civil rights heroes like Rosa Parks and Martin Luther King, Jr. and the great racial change of the mid-twentieth century.

As a nation, we owe her gratitude for showing that talent and dignity can prevail.

— Leontyne Price

How Will You Rock the World?

"My way of rocking the world is with my voice. I will write songs of love and peace and then travel around the world singing and encouraging people to love one another. I will sing to the children of the world and spread the love."

Tonya Joyce Khakazi, age 13

Sonja Henie

1912–1969 ❋ OLYMPIC FIGURE SKATER/ACTRESS ❋ NORWAY

Sonja's star power was unlike any other. It was so profound it made an indelible mark on all those it touched.

— Joseph Gourdji, who skated with Sonja in her Hollywood Ice Review

The cold wind bit her cheeks, but Sonja was skating and twirling so fast, and was so filled with excitement, her body felt like it was on fire. She was in France, competing in the first Winter Olympics ever, and she was just eleven years old! Sonja knew that her skating was unusual—she was the only person to use ballet moves, and the only woman to do athletic jumps like the male skaters. She was sure the judges would be impressed by her innovations.

As she twirled and jumped, Sonja was happy she'd chosen a short white skating dress. The long black dresses the other women skaters wore would have limited her athletic movements. At the end of her startling routine, Sonja was nervous, but proud, and thought she had a good chance of winning. But when the judges announced the scores, she was horrified—not only had she not won the competition, she had placed dead last!

Sonja was always ahead of her time, but she didn't let that stop her. The 1924 Olympics was her first and only defeat. She would go on to win more world titles and Olympic gold medals than any other skater in history and would turn her sport on its head. She was figure skating's first and biggest superstar and set the standard for the Michelle Kwans and Tara Lipinskys to come.

Blond, dimpled Sonja was born in 1912 in Oslo, Norway. Her father was an Olympic speed skater, and both parents encouraged Sonja to try many different sports. Sonja was most interested in dance, and only learned to skate at eight so she could join her friends out on the ice. But once she discovered that she could dance on her skates, Sonja fully dedicated herself to the sport. After just one year of practice, she began winning junior competitions in Oslo. By age ten, she was Norway's national champion for all ages!

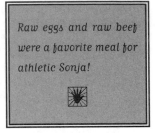

Raw eggs and raw beef were a favorite meal for athletic Sonja!

After her humiliating defeat at the Winter Olympics, Sonja vowed she would never lose again. She refused to enter any competitions the next year, and, instead, increased her training. She skated three hours in the morning and four hours in the afternoon, every single day. Her hard work paid off. In 1927, she became the youngest world champion in skating history when she was only fourteen years old! Then, in 1928, four years after her Olympic defeat, she won her first Olympic gold medal. Sonja won the gold again in 1932 and in 1936, to become figure skating's only three-time Olympic winner ever. She also successfully defended her title as World Champion for the next ten years in a row, which put her in the Guiness Book of World Records.

But, more than for her many medals, Sonja is best remembered for revolutionizing her sport. Before her, skaters just traced boring figures ("figure-eights" for example) during competition, which is why it's still called "figure skating" today. Sonja changed all that when she brought her beloved ballet to the ice. Sonja said, "Ice skating is not [just] a sport—it is an art, too. I tried to enter-

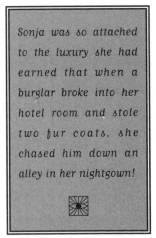

Sonja was so attached to the luxury she had earned that when a burglar broke into her hotel room and stole two fur coats, she chased him down an alley in her nightgown!

tain the public—to put some of the beauty of the dance into my skating. Now I dance on skates instead of just skating." The graceful, creative skating routines we see today are due to Sonja's revolutionary ideas.

Before Sonja came along, people thought women skaters weren't athletic enough to jump like the men. But Sonja proved that women could jump, too. She was the first woman to do a single axel jump and also developed nineteen types of spins, some of which require whirling eighty times! To free up her arms and legs, Sonja chose to wear the shorter skating dress and matching skates which set skating fashion for the next sixty years. At the time, the dress was quite shocking, since women in the 1930s didn't even show that much skin at the beach!

After more than ten years of wildly successful competition, Sonja retired to follow her other childhood dream—acting. "Ever since I was a little girl," she said, "I wanted to be on the stage." She pursued this goal as aggressively as she had skated. She moved to Hollywood and signed a lucrative contract to skate and act in movies. In 1937, her first movie, *One in a Million*, was a smash hit and Sonja followed that with eleven more successful movies. By 1939, she was one of the most popular screen stars in the world, outranked only by Shirley Temple and Clark Gable.

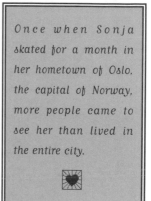

Once when Sonja skated for a month in her hometown of Oslo, the capital of Norway, more people came to see her than lived in the entire city.

During her movie career, Sonja formed her own ice show, the Hollywood Ice Review. For fifteen years, the Hollywood Ice Review toured all over the globe. It was considered the greatest box office attraction in the world! The shows drew enormous crowds, broke box office records, and even caused riots of excited fans. Once again, Sonja's dreams and ideas had changed the world of skating forever. The Ice Capades and Disney on Ice were inspired by the Hollywood Ice Review.

Thanks to her athletic and acting talents and her sharp business sense, Sonja was a millionaire by age twenty-six, earning over $50 million by the time she died in 1969, at age fifty-seven. During her lifetime, she was the world's highest-paid woman entertainer and one of the richest athletes of all time.

You know those Zamboni cars that drive onto the ice and smooth it out? Sonja discovered those, too. While touring, she saw Frank Zamboni's invention in action. She loved it so much, she got one for her show, and as she toured the world, the Zamboni caught on. Today, thousands are used in ice rinks around the world.

Eva "Evita" Perón

1919–1952 ▨ ACTRESS/POLITICIAN ▨ ARGENTINA

I should rather say that the world at the moment suffers from a lack of women. Everything, absolutely everything in this world, has been conducted on men's terms.

— Evita Perón, celebrating Argentine women winning the right to vote

A s Eva and her brothers and sisters filed past the coffin, she could feel the angry eyes of the crowd behind her burning a hole in her back. She could hardly see her dead father through her burning tears of grief and shame. When he was alive, her father had been married to another woman and had other children. Eva's mother was his mistress, and Eva and her siblings were his second, secret family. Second families were common among the rich men of Argentina, but they were objects of scorn to the upper class. In their small agricultural town, Eva and her family were outcasts.

Eva knew that her mother broke an unspoken rule by coming to the funeral. Her dead father's wealthy friends were appalled to have these poor, sinful lower-class people in their midst. In her shabby dress, Eva could feel their scorn. As the anger and shame swelled inside her, seven-year-old Eva promised herself that one day she would have their respect—one day *she* would be the one with the wealth and power.

After her lover's death, Eva's mother worried how she would take care of her family without his support. All the land and businesses were owned by a few wealthy families who refused to help out the poorer people in town. Eventually the family moved to the small town of Junín, and into a tiny, cramped apartment above an Italian restaurant. Some people say Eva's mother opened a boarding house to support her family, but others say she became a prostitute. Eva's older sisters got jobs and went to school, but Eva wasn't interested. She was star-struck and dreamed of becoming an actress. It was an impossible dream for a poor girl from the country, but Eva was not your average country girl.

In 1934, fifteen-year-old Eva left Junín for the big city—Buenos Aires— determined to be a star. Eva wasn't the only one leaving the country behind for city dreams. During the 1930s, Buenos Aires was attracting droves of poor people from the countryside who couldn't find work. Competition for jobs was severe and many people went hungry. For five long years, Eva struggled to earn a living working bit parts in stage and radio shows. Finally, just as she turned twenty, she got her first big break with a large role on a radio drama series.

Over the next few years, Eva blossomed into a star. She was making good money, so she could afford to dress more elegantly. And in the true starlet style, she dyed her brown hair blond. She also learned how to play the game of politics as well. When a military regime seized power in Argentina, Eva quickly became friends with several officers in the new government.

In 1944, at a fundraiser, Eva met the man who shared her passions for the rest of her life. Although Colonel Juan Domingo Perón arrived with a throng of beautiful women, by the end of the evening, he had eyes only for Eva. Perón was a handsome forty-eight-year-old widower who was just begin- ning to make a name for himself in politics, especially for his role in winning higher wages and benefits for lower class workers. He was drawn not only to twenty-five-year-old Eva's beauty, but also to her intelligence and ambition. But most importantly, Juan and Eva shared similar backgrounds; they were both children of forbidden relationships between a rich man and a woman of the lowest social class. Both knew how it felt to struggle against prejudices and both had worked hard for their success. They shared a mutual respect.

Just a month after they met, Perón was promoted to vice-president of a new government and Eva began doing patriotic radio shows, promoting Perón and his ideas. These shows were hugely popular and helped make Perón a household name. Eva also became president of the actors' union and more active in Perón's political decisions. At twenty-six, the once poor, lower-class girl from the country was already a millionaire.

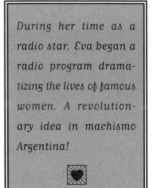

During her time as a radio star, Eva began a radio program dramatizing the lives of famous women. A revolutionary idea in machismo Argentina!

Perón and Eva became so popular and so powerful that the government felt threatened by them. Perón was arrested and Eva was fired from her radio job. The arrest only increased the couple's popularity among the poor and working-class people of Argentina, who held a daylong strike and demonstration demanding Perón's release. It brought the capital to a standstill. Perón was freed, and the lower classes felt they had won their first battle against the rich who controlled government, land, jobs—everything. The Peróns seemed like their only hope. They gave Eva the affectionate nickname by which she would always be known—"Evita."

Just after his release, Perón married Evita in a secret ceremony. He announced he would run for president, and Evita got her job back and continued promoting Perón over the radio. While most politicians were wealthy and relied on the rich, land-owning voters to get them into office, the Peróns focused on the poor and working-class voters and the trade unions for their support. Juan and Evita, with their own humble backgrounds, came to represent the poor, who were proud of who they were for the first time in Argentine history. "I feel myself responsible for the humble," said Evita, "as though I were the mother of them all."

In 1946, Perón was elected president by a large margin. At twenty-seven, Evita finally had the power she had always dreamed of. In a time when women had little power in their own homes, let alone a voice in government, Evita broke all the molds. She was determined to close the gap between the rich and the poor. She set up an office at the Ministry of Labor and forced companies to grant benefits and salary increases to workers in the trade unions. She also directed the Social Aid Foundation, raising $50 to $100 million a year to build hospitals, schools, and homes for the poor.

But Evita's greatest contribution was her fight for women's equality. At that time, women in Argentina could not vote. Evita organized rallies and gave regularly scheduled radio talks, passionately urging Congress and the people of Argentina to grant women an equal place in society. Her speeches were successful, and in 1947, Argentine women won the right to vote.

Evita also campaigned for legal rights and equal pay for women. She helped form and ran the Women's Party, through which she fought for these issues. Women were paid only half as much as men doing the same jobs. In 1949, women working in the textile industry won equal pay, and a law was passed that increased women's wages in all other jobs to 80% of men's salaries. A law was also passed that gave women legal equality in marriage and with custody of their children. Eva even went so far as to request that mothers and housewives be paid for their work!

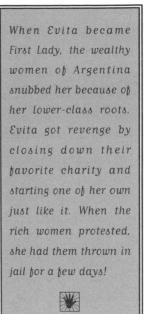

When Evita became First Lady, the wealthy women of Argentina snubbed her because of her lower-class roots. Evita got revenge by closing down their favorite charity and starting one of her own just like it. When the rich women protested, she had them thrown in jail for a few days!

In 1950, Eva shocked the country once again by announcing she would run for vice-president. Eva's triumphs, however, weren't enough to blot out the growing accusations of corruption and greed against her, Perón, and their government. Their popularity was on the decline. Public opposition was so strong that she was forced to withdraw from the race, although her husband remained on the ballot.

The years of exhausting work—of rising at eight in the morning and working until midnight—finally began to take their toll on Eva's health. Just before voters went to the polls, Evita was diagnosed with cancer. The election instantly became charged with emotion. Over 90% of eligible women voted for the first time and Perón won by a landslide.

The tarnish on Evita's reputation was virtually wiped clean, as thousands of people held prayer vigils for her recovery. She was declared "Spiritual Leader of the Nation" and "Capitana Evita." Her autobiography became an instant best-seller and required reading in all schools and universities. Despite winning back the love of her people, Evita died on July 26, 1952.

If you want to learn more about Evita's life, check out the movie starring Madonna and Antonio Banderas.

During her thirty-three years, Evita was an inspiration to the poor and working-class people of Argentina and to the women of the world. Against amazing odds, she went from a poor, illegitimate, uneducated country girl to one of the most wealthy, powerful, and revolutionary women in the world. She gave people hope that even the most unfortunate person could rise to great heights. Evita fought for the rights of those people who had no voice and forced the government to hear them, thus becoming the symbol of their hopes and dreams. For people around the world who continue to struggle against many forms of oppression in their countries, Evita is a true legend who will never be forgotten.

I want nothing for myself. My glory is and always will be . . . the banner of my people, and even if I leave shreds of my life on the wayside I know that you will gather them up in my name and carry them like a flag to victory.

— Evita Perón

How Will You Rock the World?

"I will rock the world by giving everybody who lives on the streets or in rough times a little money and support to help get their lives  back together. I would film a video of how they ended up on the streets, so others could learn from their mistakes."

Amy Ross, age 12

"I plan to become the first female president. I am determined because I feel strongly that things are breaking down and I have many ideas to make this a better world. Don't be surprised if you're watching the news one day and you see my face next to the words: 'First Female President'!"

Kara Stadelman, age 13

The Night Witches

Even if it were possible to gather and place at your feet all the flowers on earth, this would not constitute sufficient tribute to your valor. — French WWII pilots, praising the Night Witches

Marina looked out the plane's window and could see the dark forest below her. They were dropping fast and there was no place to land. The snowstorm raged around them, weighting their wings down with heavy ice and dragging them closer and closer to death.

"Lighten the plane!" yelled Valentina, who was struggling to maintain their altitude. Marina and Polina opened the hatch in the floor and threw out anything that wasn't bolted down. But it was no use—the plane kept plunging down toward the trees. When they had set out to beat a flight record, they never imagined they'd be fighting for their lives.

Suddenly, the snowstorm was *inside* the plane, as well as outside. Valentina and Polina turned to see Marina standing above the open hatch, with a fierce look on her face. She was wearing a parachute. "Don't do it, Marina! We'll never find you again in this wilderness!" they yelled. But it was too late—Marina threw herself out into the cold, dark night.

With the lighter load, they managed to keep the plane aloft until they found a clearing to land in, close to a village. Marina's remarkable courage had saved their lives. But after days of searching, they couldn't find her. She must have died alone in the woods. Ten days later, long after they and the Russian public had given up hope, a surprised hunter stumbled across Marina, freezing and half-starved, in the desolate forest.

> *The Night Witches were not the first Soviet warrior women. The legendary Amazons were also from southern Russia!*

The "Winged Sisters" received a heroes' welcome when they returned to Moscow. Tens of thousands of fans lined the streets to cheer the winners of the women's world record for a distance flight, after their dangerous 3,700-mile (6,000-km) journey across Russia. Each pilot was awarded the Gold Star of Hero of the Soviet Union, the first women to earn such an honor, but the crowds really came to see Captain Marina Raskova, the brave young woman who risked her life to save their mission.

Marina was just nineteen when she began flying and was the first woman in Russia to pass the navigator exam. She inspired thousands of girls, factory workers, and even housewives, to earn their wings after her heroic 1938 flight. She was the Amelia Earhart of Russia. Local flying clubs were set up by the government to train girls as young as seventeen, free of charge. Marina encouraged an entire generation of Russian girls to push themselves to see what they could do—girls who would soon be called on to help save their homeland from the coming war.

Marina Raskova

In June 1941, Adolf Hitler surprised Russia and the world when he launched "Operation Barbarosa," a sneak attack against the Soviet air force. German bombers destroyed squadrons of Soviet planes as they sat parked on their airfields. The unprovoked air strikes not only threw the Soviet Union into chaos, but also gave the Germans complete air superiority. Much of the Soviet Union's air force was destroyed in the attack; the country was in trouble.

The Soviet people were eager to defend themselves against this attack on their "Rodina," Mother Russia. Recruits poured in, including thousands of teenage girls who had plenty of flying experience and wanted to get to the front. At first, these girl pilots were rejected. One official's response to a girl's application was:

Things may be bad, but we're not so desperate that we're going to put little girls like you up in the skies. Go home and help your mother.[15]

But it wasn't long before Russian officials changed their tune; there simply weren't enough male pilots and crews left in Russia to challenge the Germans.

Again, it was Marina Raskova to the rescue. Promoted to major in the Soviet Air Force, she convinced the high command to let her recruit and train all-female combat units. On Radio Moscow, Marina asked for female volunteers to fight on the front lines with the men. The response was overwhelming—who wouldn't want to serve under their hero? Bags of applications arrived every day, and Marina personally interviewed thousands of hopefuls. In the end, over a thousand of the best candidates were chosen. Some got to be fighter pilots, others navigators, and the rest mechanics and support personnel. Most of the young women chosen for the elite units were still teenagers!

From the very beginning, these girls faced different obstacles than their male counterparts. The government didn't even bother to make women's uniforms, and, instead, gave them the same uniforms as the men. One female fighter remembered, "They were gigantic—vests dangled down below the knee, trousers hitched up almost to the chin, coats spilled onto the floor like bridal trains." Another said, "God knows what the Germans would have thought." And since the battle against the Germans was already underway, their training was accelerated, to say the least. The young women had to cram nearly three years of flying experience into just three months!

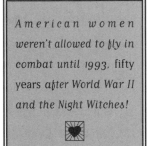

American women weren't allowed to fly in combat until 1993, fifty years after World War II and the Night Witches!

The most serious difficulty they faced, however, was the sexism of their male comrades. Many male pilots refused to fly with women "wingmen" or to go up in airplanes that had been repaired by women mechanics. Many believed that women weren't as skilled or as brave as men and had no place in the war.

The female fighters didn't let these attitudes stop them, however. The Germans had invaded their country, too, and they knew they had the skills to fight back. It didn't take long for the women to prove themselves. Like male pilots, they battled in countless aerial dogfights, bombed bridges and ammunition depots, cleared safe paths for advancing Russian soldiers, and protected Soviet military installations.

They were particularly successful in their night bombing attacks on advancing German troops. Sleep was critical for exhausted soldiers on the front lines, so the all-night terror of the attacks was devastating to the enemy. A German commander described the effect of their raids:

> *We simply couldn't grasp that the Soviet airmen that caused us the greatest trouble were in fact WOMEN. These women feared nothing. They came night after night . . . and . . . wouldn't give us any sleep at all.*[16]

In one evening, the pilots attacked eighteen times! The Germans were so afraid of the raids, they dubbed the pilots "Night Witches."

The night attacks were almost as terrifying for the pilots as well. They flew in biplanes that were normally used just for training, since they were very slow and could be seen and heard from a great distance. They were easy targets for the enemy. One female pilot tells of a particularly terrifying mission:

> *The antiaircraft guns fired at us fiercely from all directions, and suddenly I felt our aircraft hit. My foot slipped down into an empty space below me; the bottom of the cockpit had been shot away. I felt something hot streaming down my left arm and leg—I was wounded. Blinded by the searchlights . . . I was completely disoriented: the sky and earth were indistinguishable to my vision . . .*[17]

The flimsy planes were made of canvas, so, if shot, they often went up in flames. This meant almost certain death for the crew, since there were no parachutes on board! Even if they managed to land the plane, they had to be careful to land on the *Russian* side of the battle lines, so they would not be taken prisoner by the enemy.

The night witches devised risky tactics to make up for their planes. In one maneuver, a brave pilot would fly alone over the enemy camp, attracting their

floodlights and machine gun fire. As the Germans shot at the lone plane, two more pilots would glide in with their engines off and drop their bombs. Before the Germans knew what had happened, all three planes were gone. If a much faster German plane came after them, their only escape was to out-maneuver it. They often did this by flying so low to the ground that their planes were hidden by trees!

Lilya Litvak

Night Witches were so difficult to catch, in fact, that German pilots were promised an Iron Cross (the German medal of highest honor) for shooting one down.

These courageous female pilots saw at least as much action as the men. In just one all-female unit, the pilots flew in over 24,000 combat assaults during the war! They won thousands of medals and honors. In fact, twenty-nine female pilots won the prestigious "Hero of the Soviet Union" award; twenty-three of those awards went to Night Witches!

One daredevil pilot, in particular, became quite famous to the Russian public, and infamous to her German enemies—Lilya Litvak. When she was just fifteen, Lily, as she was known, tried to join her local flying club, but was told that she would have to wait two more years, like everyone else. But Lily was determined and read every aviation book she could get her hands on. She pestered instructors, displaying her incredible

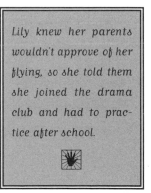

Lily knew her parents wouldn't approve of her flying, so she told them she joined the drama club and had to practice after school.

knowledge, until they gave in and let her enroll early, at age sixteen. Lily was a natural flyer, and learned much faster than other students. Soon this teenager was so good that she, too, became an instructor.

When Marina made her radio announcement for female pilots, Lily was one of the first girls to sign up for the all-female units. She was quickly promoted to fight in the dangerous battles over Stalingrad, with an all-male unit. Although Lily was extremely beautiful, she didn't let that distract her male comrades from their missions. When one young fighter confessed his love for Lily, she replied, "Let's get the fighting over first, darling—then maybe we can talk about love, eh?"

Lily quickly earned the respect of her male squad. In less than a year of combat, she flew 168 successful missions, and shot down an astounding twelve enemy planes. In recognition of her bravery, she was awarded the prestigious Order of the Red Banner and was promoted to senior lieutenant. She painted a large white rose on each side of her cockpit, plus a row of twelve smaller roses along the nose for each of her "kills," earning her the name "The White Rose of Stalingrad." When German fighters saw the White Rose coming, they would usually turn and flee, rather than fight. Over the radio, the Soviets could hear German pilots call warnings to each other as she approached, "Achtung, Litvak!"

> *It was almost impossible for female pilots to wash their hair on the freezing front lines. But Lily came up with a brilliant plan: after a day of flying, she opened her plane's radiator and drained the scalding water into a bucket. Right on the runway, she'd fling off her helmet and soap up with the only hot water to be found!*

Once Lily shot down a German plane, and the pilot parachuted out and was captured by Russian troops. When they questioned the highly-decorated Nazi, he asked to meet the pilot who had shot him down. He was surprised and angry when Lily walked in, and demanded an explanation for this Russian joke. But his anger turned to humiliation when Lily began describing their dogfight in detail, explaining exactly how she had beaten him. The German could not even look at her. "Her eyes were flashing like a tiger. She was enjoying herself," said a friend who was there.

Sadly, in August 1943, Lily's luck ran out. While scouting the front lines for enemy bombers, Lily found them. A group of German fighters distracted the other Russian planes, as eight fighters ganged up on Lily. They had seen the White Rose and weren't about to let her escape again.

> *In spite of her tough exterior, Lily loved beauty. She picked wildflowers before missions, tucking them behind her ear for good luck. Even on the day she was shot down, Lily had flowers pinned to her control panel.*

She fought back with all she had, and it took all eight German planes to hit her, but "The White Rose of Stalingrad" finally went down in flames. Lily was just twenty-two years old when she died.

Marina Raskova also died before the end of the war. In 1943, while leading two planes through a blinding snowstorm, Marina became disoriented and flew too low. She crashed into the steep bank of the Volga River and died. The female fighter pilots had seen many of their

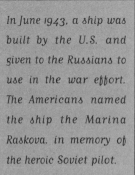

In June 1943, a ship was built by the U.S. and given to the Russians to use in the war effort. The Americans named the ship the Marina Raskova, in memory of the heroic Soviet pilot.

friends killed in battle, but losing their inspiration, their hero, was almost more than they could bear. One pilot described the reaction to Marina's death:

> *There was a moment or two of complete silence. Then it seemed that everyone was crying together. All around was the sound of the most anguished sobbing.*[18]

Although many of Russia's greatest war heroines didn't live to see their country defeat the German invaders, their courage and contributions are still celebrated. After the war, a monument was built near where Lily's plane went down to honor her as a war hero. And in 1990, Lily was still remembered by the Russian people when she finally received the "Hero of the Soviet Union" award from then prime minister, Mikhail Gorbachev. Marina and Lily would have been proud of their women comrades. The female combat units took part in some of the heaviest, most dangerous air combat in history. They refused to back down, and helped fight off the German invasion and win the war.

How Will You Rock the World?

"I am not going to rock just this world, I am going to rock the entire Milky Way! I am going to be the first female Canadian astronaut who is in a wheelchair."

Rae Bell, age 13

"I will rock the world by being an astronaut and exploring other worlds and stars. I will fly in an F-14 first, then I will go to space school."

Whitney Lang, age 8

"I want to create a stunt for planes. I will perform the stunt, along with risky turns and maneuvers, better than any other pilot. I also want to be the first pilot to test out new jets. I think flying is the best thing in the world and that's how I plan to rock it."

Leigh Delahanty, age 12

Oprah Winfrey

1954– ⊕ ACTRESS/PRODUCER ⊕ UNITED STATES

*I believe you're here
to live your life with
passion. Otherwise,
you're just traveling
through the world
blindly—and there's
no point to that.*
— Oprah Winfrey

With a young out-of-control daughter on her hands, Oprah Winfrey's mother decided that her only option was to send Oprah to live with her father, Vernon, in Nashville. She knew that Oprah was headed for trouble if she stayed in Milwaukee.

But Oprah was terrified of her father. He was the strictest person she knew and she worried about what he would do to her when he heard about the trouble she'd been in. Fourteen-year-old Oprah vowed that if she survived living with her father, she would turn her life around. She'd show them all.

No one in Oprah's family could have imagined that she was destined to become the richest entertainer in the world, when she was born on a poor Mississippi farm to a teenage single mother. Her father didn't even know she existed until he received a birth notice that said, "Send clothes!" When

Oprah's mother moved north to find work, Oprah was raised on a farm by her strict grandmother, Hattie Mae, for six years.

She began speaking at her grandmother's church when she was just three years old. Oprah had natural talent for performing and became very popular with the congregation. She loved making her grandmother proud:

> It was a way of getting love . . . the sisters sitting in the front row would fan themselves and . . . say, 'Hattie Mae, this child is gifted.'[19]

On the farm, Oprah entertained herself riding the pigs bareback and reading Bible stories out loud to the other animals.

When Oprah was six years old, her mother, Vernita, got a job as a maid in Milwaukee, Wisconsin, and finally called for her. In Milwaukee, as on the farm, Oprah was still very poor, but instead of having the outdoors and animals to comfort her, Oprah had to cram into one room with her mother and stepbrother and sister. Because of her job, Vernita left the children early in the morning and returned late at night. She didn't have much time for her family:

> Her way of showing love to me was getting out and going to work every day, putting clothes on my back, and having food on the table. At that time, I didn't understand it.[20]

Young Oprah was starved for attention.

To get her mother to notice her, Oprah started running away. When she was nine years old, she was molested by a nineteen-year-old cousin who was baby-sitting her. Oprah believed it was her fault and didn't tell anyone.

With no one to help her, Oprah's behavior spun further out of control. By the time she was fourteen, she was pregnant (the baby died shortly after birth) and, as Oprah puts it, "was definitely headed for a career as a juvenile delinquent." When Oprah ran away for a week, Vernita decided she could no longer handle her child. That's when she sent her to live with her father in Nashville.

Vernon Winfrey, and his wife, Zelma, were respected members of their Tennessee community. Vernon was a barber, store owner, city councillor, and church official. He didn't put up with Oprah's negative attitude or bad grades, and his word was law. He told rebellious Oprah his philosophy on obedience: "If I tell you a mosquito can pull a wagon, don't ask me no questions. Just hitch him up."

It was obvious Oprah was a smart girl, so Vernon demanded she work up to her potential. She had been getting Cs in Milwaukee, but only As were acceptable to her father. Every week, he and Zelma made Oprah write book reports, besides doing her school homework, and they quizzed her on new vocabulary words. At first she hated their strict rules and high expectations, but it turned out to be just what she needed—parents who made rules and enforced them, but who also gave her the love and attention she craved. Oprah blossomed.

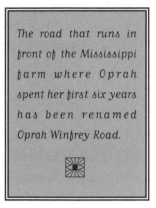

The road that runs in front of the Mississippi farm where Oprah spent her first six years has been renamed Oprah Winfrey Road.

Not only did her grades skyrocket, she also became more outgoing and popular than she'd ever been before. In high school she was chosen to represent her school at a White House youth conference and won a $1,000 scholarship for a speech she wrote, "The Negro, the Constitution, and the United States." Her father encouraged Oprah to dream big, and that she did. At sixteen, she traveled to Los Angeles to speak at a church. When she returned, she told Vernon that someday her handprints would be next to the other stars' outside Mann's Chinese Theatre.

Oprah the teenager was full of self-confidence. At seventeen, she landed her first show biz job, as a newscaster for a local radio station. They even paid her a hundred dollars a week, big money to a high school kid in the 1970s. She kept the job even after she won a scholarship to Tennessee State University and started college. But by nineteen, she had been discovered by a Nashville TV station and was hired as a reporter and news anchor. A boyfriend remembered Oprah during this time:

> She knew what she wanted very early in life. She said she wanted to be an actress. She worked hard at it, and when her ship started to sail, she got aboard.[21]

Oprah was on her way.

Her rise to superstardom was steady. In 1976, she became a TV anchor in Baltimore, then was promoted to co-host of a morning talk show called *People*

Are Talking. Her producers felt Oprah's looks needed some improving, and in spite of her self-confidence, she let them thin her hair. When she went temporarily bald from their "beauty treatment," she vowed she'd never let other people tell her how to be beautiful again.

The talk show format was perfect for Oprah—audiences loved her humor, honesty, and down-to-earth personality—and her ratings soared. In 1984, Oprah got her big break; she was asked to host her own show in a major city. *A.M. Chicago* aired at the same time as the popular *Phil Donahue Show.* He was the king of daytime TV, but it wasn't long before Oprah dethroned him. Soon she was a star in 120 cities across America. *The Oprah Winfrey Show* made its national debut in 1986 and was an instant hit, becoming one of the most popular shows on television. Even more incredible, this black woman who rose from poverty and abuse became the highest-paid person in show business—male or female, black or white!

Oprah has turned her show into a platform for educating people and fighting for her causes. Inspired by her childhood love of reading (and perhaps by all those book reports!), she started "Oprah's Book Club." Although people in the industry thought it was risky, the club has become hugely popular. Now, when Oprah chooses a book, it practically guarantees that it will become an instant bestseller! Other childhood events also influenced her. In 1990, the Year of the Child, Oprah did at least one show a month on children's issues, and, in 1991, it took all her strength to talk about her own abuse on the air. But she did it, hoping to help other victims find the courage to speak out and get counseling.

> Oprah was supposed to be named Orpah, from the book of Ruth in the Bible, but the hospital misspelled her name on her birth certificate.

Through her show, Oprah continually inspires others to get involved and make a difference. In 1997, she started "The Angel Network," which encourages viewers to make the world a better place. Viewers working with the network have raised millions of dollars for college scholarships and have built hundreds of homes with Habitat for Humanity. Every week, Oprah gives $50,000 to people who are using their lives to improve the lives of others, to help them expand their programs and do even more for those in need.

Oprah is active outside her show, as well. She founded the "Little Sisters" program in a Chicago housing project, to give counseling to young girls; she lobbies Washington on child abuse issues; and she set up a $750,000 scholarship at Tennessee State University. She also realized her childhood dream of being a movie star, acting in dramas by some of the most brilliant black writers of our time: *The Color Purple, Native Son, The Women of Brewster Place, Before Women Had Wings,* and *Beloved.* She even formed her own TV and movie company, Harpo Productions (that's Oprah backwards), to help get important projects onto the screen—usually projects that empower women and girls to be strong and tough.

Oprah's dedication and compassion have won her countless awards, including Woman of Achievement, Broadcaster of the Year, Entertainer of the Year, a George Foster Peabody Award and Lifetime Achievement Award from the National Academy of TV Arts and Sciences, thirty-three Emmys, and Golden Globe and Academy Award nominations.

Oprah's father used to say, "There are those who make things happen. There are those who watch things happen, and there are those that don't know what's happening." Oprah sure chose to make things happen.

More meaningful than her awards, however, is the model Oprah sets for people. Rather than let her own traumatic childhood hold her back, Oprah used her experiences to motivate her. Instead of blaming others for her past or using it as an excuse to give up, Oprah encourages others to take responsibility for *overcoming* their past. "You have to be responsible for claiming your own victories," she says, "If you live in the past and allow the past to define who you are then you never grow." Oprah never let anyone or anything define who she is, and she continues to inspire millions of people every day.

> *I feel so strongly that my life is to be used as an example to show people what can be done.*
> — Oprah Winfrey

How Will You Rock the World?

"I want to be the kind of actress that makes people say, 'A new movie just came out with Jasmine Jacobs in it, so it <u>must</u> be good.' I am going to rock the world by being the best actress the world has ever seen. So watch out, Mary Kate and Ashley, 'cause here comes Jasmine!"

Jasmine Jacobs, age 11

"I want to be a comedy star. I love making people laugh and smile."

Whitney Prentiss, age 12

Rigoberta Menchu

1959– ❀ *POLITICAL ACTIVIST* ❀ *GUATEMALA*

Rigoberta Menchu appeals to the best in all of us, wherever we live and whatever our background.
— the Nobel Peace Prize Committee

Rigoberta's back ached as she bent to pick up the beans that had fallen off the coffee bushes. Up ahead, she could see her mother picking, with her baby brother, Nicholás, strapped to her back. Rigoberta was worried. They had been at this *finca* (large coffee, cotton, or sugar cane plantation) for fifteen days now, and Nicholas had been crying the whole time. He was crying now. Her mother unwrapped him and tried to feed him some healing herbs. His belly was swollen from malnutrition and he was barely breathing.

Eight-year-old Rigoberta could hardly contain her anger. Working on the *fincas*, they could hardly afford to buy food, let alone medicine for a sick baby. They couldn't ask for help because they spoke a different language than the other workers. But most unfair was that if her mother stopped working to care for Nicholás, they would all be thrown out and would lose the money they desperately needed for food. When Nicholás died later that morning, Rigoberta was angrier than she'd ever been in her entire life. The day of his death was the first day of her battle to save her Indian people from their tremendous struggles.

Rigoberta Menchu was born in 1959, in the mountains of northwest Guatemala. She and her seven siblings grew up in the village of Chimel, which her parents founded. Like most of the people in Guatemala, Rigoberta's family and village were descended from the ancient and proud Mayan Indians of Central America. The families in her village were very poor, living in small huts built from cane or corn stalks. The villagers spent years clearing fields out of the forest, just to grow enough corn to feed their families. But most years they couldn't live off their meager crops, so they were forced to work on the *fincas* that were owned by the *ladinos* (people descended from the Spanish who had invaded in the 1500s).

Although most Guatemalans are Indian, it was the *ladinos* who controlled most of the country's land and businesses. Like most Indian children, Rigoberta never had a chance to go to school. As soon as she could walk, Rigoberta helped her parents at the *fincas*. She picked up fallen coffee or cotton behind her mother, or watched her younger siblings so her mother could pick more. By age eight, Rigoberta was working full-time. Full-time meant from three in the morning until the sun went down! For her fifteen-hour day she was paid about four cents!

Conditions were terrible. Although workers earned just enough to stay alive, the *finca* owners would cut their pay if they broke a branch off a coffee bush. They could buy extra food, medicine, and other necessities at the company store, but for much higher prices than normal. The result was that many workers earned no money at all after their months of hard labor, and many actually went into debt to pay for food. Workers who complained were fired. Rigoberta lost two brothers on the *fincas*; the younger one who died of

> At Rigoberta's birth, a midwife tied red thread around her hands and feet, to symbolize her purity and remind her to care for the earth. Around Rigoberta's neck, she tied a small red pouch, containing herbs, plants, salt, lime, tobacco, and garlic, to protect the girl from harm.

malnutrition, and an older one who died from being sprayed with toxic pesticides (*finca* owners usually didn't clear workers from the fields while they sprayed).

When the families returned to their mountain villages to work their own fields, they faced even more difficult problems. They spent years clearing land and tending fields before they would finally produce enough to feed the families. That's just when the rich landowners stepped in, claiming the land was really theirs. The Indians would have to leave or work on the land as laborers.

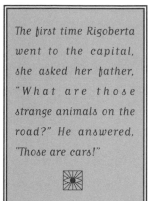

The first time Rigoberta went to the capital, she asked her father, "What are those strange animals on the road?" He answered, "Those are cars!"

As village leader, Rigoberta's father, Vicente, protested. Rigoberta often traveled with him to the capital, Guatemala City, where he met with members of the government and asked for help. They didn't care about the problems of the Indians, so Vicente met with labor organizations that really were trying to help the workers. Rigoberta came to believe that the only way the Indians could protect themselves from the government and the rich landowners would be to organize and fight for their rights. Rigoberta's father encouraged her. He often told her, "When you are old enough, you . . . must do what I do."

Her father was first arrested for his role in organizing the Indians when Rigoberta was just thirteen. Over the next few years, life became a nightmare. The government and landowners sent armies into villages. They destroyed everything, killing men, women, and children. They imprisoned and tortured anyone who fought back. They even forced young Indian men to fight against their own people, or be killed.

When Vicente first went to the government for help, they tricked him into signing papers written in Spanish, which he couldn't read, saying that the Indians would give their land to the landowners.

By the time she was fifteen, Rigoberta had taken over as a leader of her people. She met with her father's friends, priests, and Europeans. She organized her own village to protect itself from army raids. Of course, there was no money for defense, but they were creative. They developed underground escape routes, secret hideouts, and booby traps. The villagers learned to defend themselves with sticks, rocks and other crude weapons.

Once her own village was prepared, Rigoberta began traveling to other villages to teach them to fight back. As she traveled, she began to realize that the biggest obstacle keeping Indians from organizing was their language. The Mayan Indians spoke twenty-two different languages, and few people spoke Spanish, so communicating with each other and protesting Spanish laws were nearly impossible. Over the next few years, Rigoberta learned to speak three other main Mayan languages, and she improved her Spanish with the help of the Catholic nuns in the villages. She now had the tools she needed to be the voice of her people.

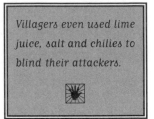

Villagers even used lime juice, salt and chilies to blind their attackers.

By 1978, when she was nineteen, Rigoberta and her entire family were being hunted by the government. They were all involved in fighting for Indian rights. Earlier her father had helped start the Committee of Peasant Unity, or CUC, which fought for fair wages and decent treatment from the landowners, and demanded respect for Indian communities, religion, and culture. When Rigoberta joined the CUC in 1979, it had grown into a powerful political group, supported by the majority of Guatemalans.

It was too dangerous for the entire family to stay together, so the village had a special fiesta to honor the Menchu family and to say goodbye. They ate a feast of roast pig and tamales, played drums and marimbas, and danced late into the night. It was one of the happiest memories of Rigoberta's difficult life. The next morning, they all scattered to different villages. It was the last time Rigoberta would see her family together and alive.

First her younger brother, Petrocinio, was tortured and burned to death while Rigoberta and her mother watched helplessly. Four months later, her father was killed during a protest in the capital. He and other CUC members took over several radio stations, trying to broadcast their story to the outside world. When they took over the Spanish embassy, still trying to get the world's attention, the army bombed the building. Everyone inside died. Finally, the next year, Rigoberta's mother was kidnapped and killed while out buying food for hungry villagers.

The Indian people of Guatemala now looked to Rigoberta to guide them. She became a leader of the CUC, organizing more protests in the capital and self-defense workshops in the villages. Everywhere Rigoberta went, she was hunted. The kidnappings and killings continued. By 1980, 100,000 Indians had been killed, 30,000 were missing, and another 200,000 had fled to Mexico. In 1981, at age twenty-two, Rigoberta, fearing for her life, joined her people in exile. She fled to Mexico. It broke her heart to leave her struggling people behind, but it was the only way she could spread their story to the outside world. If she did, she knew she could get the help the Indians needed to survive.

In Mexico she led the efforts to stop Guatemala's brutal treatment of the Indians. She began traveling the world telling of her people's struggle. Finally, in 1983, the whole world heard the voice of the Guatemalan Indians, through the publication of *I, Rigoberta Menchu*, a book about Rigoberta's life. It was a huge hit and was published in twelve languages. In 1992, the little girl who had picked coffee beans off the ground won the Nobel Peace Prize for her efforts on behalf of her people. She was the youngest person ever to win the world's most prestigious prize.

Thanks to Rigoberta's leadership and the courage of her people, conditions in Guatemala have improved. She used the $1.2 million Nobel award to start the Vicente Menchu Foundation. Its mission is to continue helping native peoples improve their communities. With the world's outraged attention focused on Guatemala, the government was forced to stop most of its attacks and kidnappings. Recent governments have worked with Rigoberta and Indian groups to address their concerns.

With Guatemala's problems improving, Rigoberta finally felt she could spare enough of herself to fall in love and get married, something she thought she would never do. But Rigoberta has not rested. Instead, she has turned her atten-

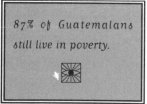

87% of Guatemalans still live in poverty.

tion to the indigenous (native) peoples all over the world. "We have broken the silence around Guatemala. Now I would like to see native and non-native people living side by side," she said. In 1993, Rigoberta was chosen by the United Nations to be a Goodwill Ambassador for the Indigenous Peoples. Her own organization, the Rigoberta Menchu Foundation, promotes peace, human rights, the rights and values of indigenous peoples, the rights of women and children, and sustainable, socially conscious development of the third world.

Rigoberta's work is far from finished. As long as there is injustice, Rigoberta will continue to be the brave voice of the oppressed, impoverished peoples of the world.

How Will You Rock the World?

"I will rock the world by becoming a forensic anthropologist. I will study the bones of the dead to help police crack baffling cases and bring murderers to justice. I can also learn things about our ancestors and teach it to others."

Megan Bailey, age 12

"My #1 dream is to become a lawyer who is known around the world. I like helping people and that's what lawyers do. I will help people fight for justice and their rights."

Jamie Kucsera, age 11

"I will rock the world by teaching children with special needs. My brother has a special need and I want to help children like him."

Mara Gomes, age 11

Maya Lin

1959– ✹ ARCHITECT ✹ UNITED STATES

You cannot ever forget that war is not just a victory or loss. It's really about individual lives.
— Maya Lin, discussing her design for the Vietnam Memorial

Professor Burr talked on and on. Maya loved her architecture class and thought Burr was brilliant, but some days her mind wandered—especially on beautiful spring days like this one. The students rustled in their chairs when a stranger entered the lecture hall and handed a message to the professor. As he read it, his face changed. A look of shock swept across his features. He cleared his throat and made an announcement.

"The Vietnam War veterans have chosen their winner for the memorial competition..."

Maya and the other students wondered why they brought this message to class. They had all entered a design into the contest for a new national monument in Washington, D.C. to honor Vietnam veterans. It was a class assignment, but everyone knew a professional architect would win, not a student. Why not let them read about the winner in the newspaper, like everyone else?

"... and the winner is our own Maya Lin!"

The entire room gasped, including Maya. How could it be? Maya was just a college senior, with no real architecture experience. Her design was strange, unlike any memorials the students had ever seen. In fact, Professor Burr had given her a B for her work. And yet she had won over almost 1,500 entries.

Professor Burr walked up to Maya and shook her hand.

"Congratulations, Maya," he said cheerfully, trying to hide his disappointment. He, too, had entered the contest. This young, inexperienced student had beaten him.

This was the first day of Maya's professional architecture career. She would go on to design some of the most original and beloved monuments in America. But her passion for designing and building began when she was a much younger girl.

Maya's parents fled China in the late 1940s. Her mother left with just one hundred-dollar bill pinned to the lining of her jacket. When they arrived in America, both were hired by Ohio University; her father became an art professor, and her mother worked as a professor of Oriental and English literature. Once settled in Athens, Ohio, they had a son and then a daughter, Maya.

Maya and her brother grew up on the college campus, in a stimulating, artistic environment. "My parents very much brought us up to decide what we wanted to," Maya said, "maybe that is an Eastern philosophy—that you don't force an opinion on a child." Later in life, Maya explored many career directions, but even as a young girl she was fascinated by architecture. She spent many hours in her room building miniature towns out of paper and scraps from her father's art studio.

When Maya graduated from high school, she was accepted at Yale University, where she studied architecture and sculpture. Her professors wanted her to choose one or the other, but Maya refused. She felt that learning about sculpture improved her architecture skills and vice-versa:

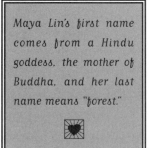

Maya Lin's first name comes from a Hindu goddess, the mother of Buddha, and her last name means "forest."

Architecture . . . is like writing a book. Everything in a building matters, from the doorknobs to the paint details. And sculpture is like writing a poem. You're not saying as much. It's an idea stripped bare.[22]

Even now, Maya still uses sculpture to create her architectural designs. First, she builds tiny models, then makes detailed drawings from those models.

During her junior year, Maya studied architecture in Europe. She noticed that Europeans went to the beautiful, park-like cemeteries not just to mourn, but also to enjoy the peaceful surroundings. They went there to relax and escape from the busy cities. "I've always been intrigued by death," she explained, "and man's reaction to it." She realized that death was all around, and people had to find ways to deal with their grief and find peace.

Back at Yale for her senior year, Maya put her insights to good use on an intriguing class assignment—to design a memorial honoring those who died in the Vietnam War. The winning design would be built in the Constitutional Gardens of Washington, D.C. There were only two requirements for the design: 1) the names of the 58,000 soldiers killed or missing in action should be included, and 2) it should be in harmony with the landscape (it would go between the Lincoln Memorial and the Washington Monument). The selection committee also hoped the design would help America heal the pain of this controversial war.

Before starting on her entry, Maya walked around Constitution Gardens, studying every detail of the location. She asked herself questions like, "How can the relatives of people killed in Vietnam recover from their loss?" and "How can America recover from the war?" Her answer was to create a design that would encourage people to look at their pain, admit to their losses, and always remember the war and those who died in it. The design Maya turned in was of two long, black granite walls joined at the center in a 130-degree angle—it looked a bit like two sides of a triangle. Every soldier's name would be carved into the walls, but the shiny black granite would reflect the image of the viewer. It was as if by looking at the names, visitors would be examining themselves. Since other D.C. monuments were generally realistic statues of people, Maya's design was unusual, to say the least.

When she first beat out the 1,420 other entries, people were excited that a young woman had won, but her design quickly became a flashpoint for America's still conflicted emotions about the war. Some people liked

Maya's haunting sculpture, but others were upset that it didn't look like a patriotic war memorial "should" look. The *Chicago Tribune* said it was "bizarre" and *The New York Times* called it "a black gash of shame."

Powerful men in Washington began speaking out against Maya's entry; Interior Secretary James Watt, Texas billionaire Ross Perot, and Senator Jeremiah Denton all fought to stop the project. They were not excited about Maya's

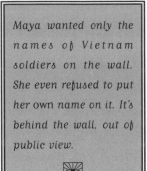

Maya wanted only the names of Vietnam soldiers on the wall. She even refused to put her own name on it. It's behind the wall, out of public view.

unique vision. In fact, one big complaint was that all the other Washington monuments were white but this one was black. They even criticized Maya, complaining that since she was a young woman who didn't fight in Vietnam, she couldn't possibly understand the meaning of the war.

In spite of the public conflict, Maya defended her design and refused to change it. She knew the public would respond to it if it were built. Jan Scruggs, the veteran who led the drive to create the memorial, said of Maya's courage, "She really believed in this design . . . the strength of her own convictions carried us through quite a few conflicts." Against Maya's wishes, a compromise was reached; a second memorial would be built near Maya's site. It was a traditional statue of three soldiers, designed by Frederick Hart. Hart was paid $200,000 for his design; Maya was paid $20,000.

When her wall was finally built in 1982, it became an overnight sensation. The critics were silenced. Finally, the nation had a focus for thirty years of unresolved grief and anger over Vietnam. The reflective sculpture encouraged

visitors to deal with their repressed emotions about Vietnam, and helped everyone grieve. Visitors leave flowers and momentos below the names of loved ones and even make pencil impressions of the names onto paper to take home with them. The award committee praised its impact, "This one superb design has changed the way war memorials—and monuments as a whole—are perceived." Maya was honored with

Visitors are often surprised at how warm the Wall is to the touch—as if it was alive (the black granite holds the warmth of the sun).

the 1988 Presidential Design Award, but more important to her, the Vietnam Memorial is now the most-visited memorial in the United States.

After the Wall, Maya vowed never to do another memorial because of the controversy she had endured over the Vietnam Memorial. But when she was asked to design the Civil Rights Memorial, she couldn't refuse. The monument honors the people who fought for equality during the Civil Rights movement of the 1950s and 1960s, from well-known leaders like Rosa Parks and Martin Luther King, Jr. to forgotten heroes. Maya studied history books and the speeches of Dr. King to

Maya's sculptures take one to two years to complete and sell for $6,000 to $12,000 each.

come up with another innovative design, a black granite wall carved with a quote from Dr. King and covered by a thin sheet of water flowing over it into a pool. In front of the wall is a large black granite disk inscribed with a chronology of events during the Civil Rights era, from the outlawing of school segregation to the assassination of Dr. King.

Maya continues to work as an architect, and has added many new memorials and public sculptures to her portfolio. Her designs never overpower the audience or the space. Their goal is not to intimidate or to lecture, but to inspire people to stop and think. She wants her work to stir emotions in people. The Vietnam Memorial has not only stirred the emotions of hundreds of thousands of visitors, it has also helped Americans come to terms with their conflicting emotions about the war and heal its wounds. Although Maya is still very young and plans to contribute much more, she has already left her mark on the world—a mark of peace and reconciliation.

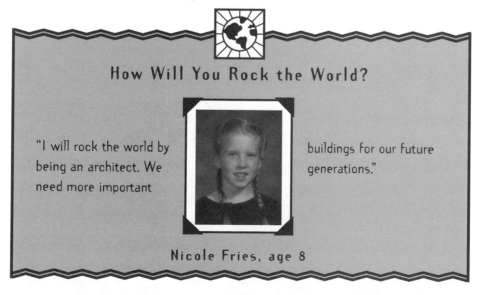

How Will You Rock the World?

"I will rock the world by being an architect. We need more important buildings for our future generations."

Nicole Fries, age 8

Lynn Hill

1961– ❧ ROCK CLIMBER ❧ UNITED STATES

The way you approach [a climb], your attitude and spirit, are reflections of how you deal with life . . . I'm basically an optimist, and I like challenges. When people say, 'It can't be done,' or 'You don't have what it takes,' it makes the task all the more interesting.

— Lynn Hill

Her sister was tying knots and explaining how to make a harness, but Lynn was staring up at the rock they were about to climb. The beautiful slab of granite was reflecting different colors as the sunlight hit it. When Lynn was ready to begin the first climb of her life, strapped into her harness and tied to the rope, she put her hands on the rock and was surprised to find that it was warm. It felt alive.

Although her sister was older and an experienced climber, fourteen-year-old Lynn was stronger and more agile. They decided that Lynn would lead the climb, and her sister would follow. By going first, Lynn would have no one to watch to get ideas on holds or techniques for getting up the rock. She'd be totally on her own. Her sister didn't offer any advice, either; she just pointed up and said, "O.K., now go."

And go she did. Lynn scaled the rock like she'd been doing it her whole life. She loved the way the granite felt under her body, she loved the fresh air, the stunning views, having some quiet space all to herself, and she loved figuring out each move on her own. When she reached the top of the rock, she looked back down and thought, "Wow, that was *intense!*" Every muscle in her body was shaking. She felt totally alive.

From that day on, Lynn was completely addicted to her new sport. She would go from being a novice teenage climber to a world-class star—the best woman climber in the world. But she never did it for the glory or the lucrative endorsements. Lynn climbs because she loves it.

She grew up in Orange County, California, and even as a young child, she seemed to have a passion for climbing. Her mother wrote in her baby book, "Lynn climbs the monkey bars like a pro." She was a small but athletic girl, and gymnastics was her chosen sport until the day her older sister took her "rock climbing." Back in 1975, rock climbing wasn't really considered a sport; it was more something that outsiders or radicals, did for fun. Women climbers, let alone girls, were rare, but that didn't stop Lynn as she began her ascent of the rock climbing world.

From the very beginning, Lynn realized she would have to listen to her own voice on what she *could* and *couldn't* do. When Lynn was fourteen, an older male climber watched her scale a particularly difficult stretch. After she finished, he gave her what he thought was a compliment, "Gee, *I* can't even do that," but Lynn was offended. Why would he assume that if *he* couldn't do it, it must be too hard for a girl? She quit listening to what other people said.

In 1979, at age nineteen, she broke her first record by climbing Ophir Broke in Colorado. It was ranked 5.12/5.13—a more difficult climb than

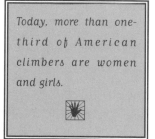

Today, more than one-third of American climbers are women and girls.

any woman had done before. Before Lynn, only men had climbed rocks with that rating. When she heard that some top male climbers were saying a woman would never be able to climb a 5.14, Lynn made it her mission to prove them wrong. In 1990, she conquered Masse Critique, in France, becoming the first woman to climb a 5.14.

While she was breaking records, Lynn was also deciding what to do with her life. In 1985, she graduated from college with a biology degree and considered becoming a physical therapist. "I didn't imagine that it was going to be possible to make a living as a professional rock climber," she admits. But climbing was her passion, and she couldn't shake it, so she worked as a guide, teaching people or leading them up routes they'd never done. As the sport became more popular, climbing competitions started. By the late 1980s, Lynn was able to make a name and a living for herself as the best female rock climber in America. In fact, she was considered one of the nation's top climbers, male or female.

In the 1990s, rock climbing really burst onto the scene, going from an experts-only club to a popular sport with almost 5 million climbers. Even people in New York City were climbing in rock gyms! Lynn rode the wave of popularity, winning climbing prizes and product endorsements.

But she still battled some prejudice in the climbing world. The problem was her size. Lynn is tiny—just 5 feet 2 inches (157 cm) tall and weighing only 100 pounds (35 kilograms). Many people thought that would be a disadvantage to her. How could she reach far away handholds? What about her strength? But Lynn soon proved, once and for all, that she could do anything she set her mind to. Her body could work to her advantage.

A climb's difficulty is ranked by the Yosemite Decimal System: 1 is trail hiking, 2 is scrambling, 3 is a steep slope, 4 is a steep slope requiring a rope, and 5 is rock climbing with a rope and other protection. A climb ranked 5.1 would be the easiest and a 5.13 would be the most difficult. The little letters next to a number (5.13a) indicates that aids are used. A 5.14 is the highest rating for now— climbing doesn't get any harder! Yet.

In 1993, Lynn secured her spot as a legend when she climbed "The Nose" of El Capitan in Yosemite National Park. This 3,000-foot (915-meter) rock face is the largest hunk of granite in the world (It's twice the size of the Sears Tower, the tallest skyscraper in America!),

In 1994, Lynn beat her own record, climbing The Nose in twenty-three straight hours!

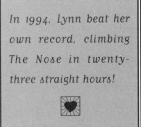

and no one, male or female, had ever been able to climb it without "aid." That is, previous climbers had been able to do it only by using equipment stuck into the rock to rest and climb on. Over an exhausting four days, Lynn became the first person to ever scale The Nose using just her own strength. And no one has been able to do it since.

Of her world-record feat, Lynn is most proud of what it says to people about their abilities:

> I think that The Nose climb actually was a statement for me about people doing what they're capable of, no matter what the perceived difficulties are. If you're small, if you're tall . . . whatever your body type or sex. It doesn't really matter. Why be limited by what other people say?[23]

Lynn now travels the world as a member of the legendary North Face Team, climbing and promoting the sport. She also designs a line of clothing for women and is writing a book about her experiences. But Lynn is more than just a rock-jock. Climbing has changed her life, and as a spokesperson for the sport, she hopes to inspire others with what she's learned. Climbing has taught her to take responsibility for her actions: "When you step off the ground on a climb . . . you have to deal with everything that comes your way and you're responsible for every movement. You can't blame anyone else." By owning up to your failures and successes, Lynn believes you gain power and self-esteem.

Lynn's been invited to the White House to honor and thank her for her contributions to women's sports.

Climbing has also shown her that materialism isn't all it's cracked up to be; there's more to life than working and buying. When she's up on a rock, she can see what's really important in life: "What's meaningful is your relationships with people and your knowledge of yourself," she says, "and climbing brings you that."

Lynn believes that climbing is a great sport for girls and women because it teaches self-assurance, problem-solving, and determination. She has certainly shown that you don't have to be a brawny stud to be the best in the world, and describes her sport as "a combination of grace and power . . .

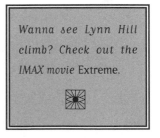

Wanna see Lynn Hill climb? Check out the IMAX movie Extreme.

You can use your own attributes to be a great climber." Over the last two decades, Lynn has used her attributes to become the very face of rock climbing. She has brought the sport to a new level of popularity and broken so many records that she is considered a legend in her own time. She continues to be an inspiration, not just to women and girls, but to *all* climbers.

How Will You Rock the World?

"I will rock the world by opening a museum about girls' sports. Most people don't think girls can do some sports. But girls can do anything that they want. I think the museum will inspire girls to rock the world in anything they do."

Samantha Daniels, age 13

"I like to play soccer and my best friend likes to play basketball, so we would open Basketsock Camp, where we'd give tips on both sports."

Bethany Thompson, age 13

"I will be the first woman to play in the NFL and I'll donate most of my money to the homeless. If that doesn't rock the world, what does?!?"

Hailey Mattson, age 11

Mia Hamm

1972– ❋ SOCCER STAR ❋ UNITED STATES

*We want to get girls out
to the games. We want
them to see the chemistry
and the intensity. Our
success is as a team, not
me as an individual.*
— Mia Hamm, praising
Team USA

"**N**ow don't tell me which one she is," he snapped. "Let me guess."
Anson Dorrance, coach of the women's national soccer team, was
sure his friend had been exaggerating when he raved about an out-of-this-world
fourteen-year-old. But here he was at a high school game to see for himself. If
Mia Hamm was that good, he'd be able to pick her out of the crowd.

No sooner did the game begin than a petite brunette burst from the crowd
and powered up the field with the ball, dodging and weaving through defen-
dants, right for the goal. Anson sucked in his breath. Could that be her? But
she dominated the entire field. How could a high-school freshman be so

good? Mia was much better than his friend claimed. Better than he would have ever dreamed. He had to get her for the national team.

The girl who would one day become the greatest female soccer player on the planet, the "big gun" of Team USA, was born on a military base in Selma, Alabama in 1972. Her father was an Air Force pilot, so Mia and her five siblings moved a lot, spending time in California, Texas, Virginia and Italy. In Italy, a country where soccer is practically worshiped, the entire family fell in love with the game and little Mia discovered her life's passion.

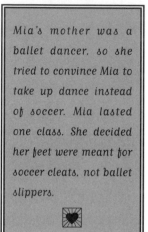

Mia's mother was a ballet dancer, so she tried to convince Mia to take up dance instead of soccer. Mia lasted one class. She decided her feet were meant for soccer cleats, not ballet slippers.

When she was five, the family moved to Texas, and Mia began playing soccer with her family. She loved to play, but hated losing, so if things weren't going her way, she'd just quit. Her siblings got fed up with this routine and refused to let her play unless she stuck it out. She never quit again. When she was old enough to play on school teams, Mia's practice paid off; she could run circles around the competition. She was able to easily dribble, dodge players, and score, while most players were still learning how to kick the ball with the inside of their foot. Off the field, Mia was very shy. Fortunately, playing soccer allowed her to express herself and her skills. Her confidence grew.

Mia was first scouted when she was just fourteen. As a freshman, she was already the best player on the girls' varsity soccer team. She was even better than every player on the guys' varsity team! In fact, she was the top female player in all of Texas! It's no surprise that Anson Dorrance, coach of the top college soccer team for women, the University of North Carolina Tar Heels, heard about Mia's incredible talents. When he went to Texas to see her play, he was blown away. She was a star, but, more importantly, she was also a team player.

He recruited her for the U.S. National Team, and at age fifteen, she was the youngest woman ever to play on it. She joined the best players in the nation. It was a whole new level of competition for Mia, a whole new level of training. "When I first did fitness with the national team, I thought I would die," she recalled. "I would cry half the time." But she stuck it out and proved herself to be one of the top midfielders in the nation.

After the thrill of her first national tournament, Mia knew what she wanted to do with her life. She told her parents she would earn a soccer scholarship to the UNC and someday she'd win the world championship. Trouble was, a world championship for women's soccer didn't exist. There was a world soccer championship only for men. But Mia didn't let that little hurdle slow her down. She finished high school by being selected as an All-American soccer player two years in a row and continued playing on the national team.

College brought more trophies and broken records. As Coach Dorrance had hoped, Mia turned out to be the UNC star player, helping the Tar Heels win NCAA championships all four years. She was the team's all-time leading scorer. In fact, Mia scored more goals than any other college soccer player in history. Proving she has the heart of a true team player, she also broke the record for number of assists. Mia alternated between earning Player of the Year and Most Valuable Player. She also won the Hermann Award as the nation's top female athlete. Her jersey, #19, was retired after her graduation.

In 1991, Mia's high school dream came true. During her freshman year at UNC, FIFA, the world soccer organization, finally decided it was time to start a World Cup for women. The first Women's World Championship soccer match would be held in China. Once again, at age nineteen, Mia was the youngest player on Team USA. After months of intense training and qualifying games, the team was up against its toughest opponents, the Norwegians (who were favored to win), in the final game. Team USA shocked the world when it beat the Norwegians and became the new world champs.

> Mia is so good that teams often put several defenders on her at once, trying to slow her down. It's common for Mia to get fouled five times or more in one game!

Four years later, Mia and her team met their first major disappointment. At the 1995 Women's World Cup, so many players on the team were injured, Mia had to play goalkeeper! Mia won Most Valuable Player for her valiant efforts, but Team USA finished a disappointing third place. Their setback, however, was a great motivator, and they doubled their efforts to prepare for the upcoming Olympics. The first year women's soccer was recognized as an Olympic sport was 1996. Mia and her team didn't want to let their country down. The Americans played in front of 76,000 screaming fans, against the hard-to-beat Chinese team. Even though they were the under-dogs, Team USA beat the odds and won the game 2-1, taking home the first gold medal for women's soccer.

The wins and glory continued. Mia went on to play in two more Olympic games, winning another gold and a silver. Team USA's stunning 1999 World Cup victory solidified its international dominance and Mia's star power. She was named U.S. Soccer's Female Athlete of the Year for 1994-1998, a record five years in a row. Mia was not only the all-time top scorer in the history of U.S. soccer, she was the best female soccer player in the world.

Perhaps not as mean-ingful to her as her Olympic gold medals, Mia was voted one of People magazine's "50 Most Beautiful People."

In the middle of Mia's meteoric rise to fame, catastrophe hit her family. Her older brother Garrett was diagnosed with a rare blood disease, aplastic anemia. A bone marrow transplant was his only chance of surviving. Because he was adopted, Mia's marrow was not a match, but she used her fame to advertise for volunteer donors. Miraculously, she did find a donor, but her brother died of complications soon after the transplant. Mia was devastated. "I'd give up all of this in a heartbeat to have him back," Mia said of her fame. "Now, no matter where I play, I feel Garrett is there."

Like a true champion, Mia didn't let her tragedy overcome her. She started the Mia Hamm Foundation to raise funds for bone marrow research and for programs that encourage girls to get involved in sports.

Mia has already left a legacy in the soccer world, breaking practically every record and helping make the sport more popular in the United States. She is a big reason why millions of girls across America are practicing their headers and slide tackles right now. Mia has inspired the next generation, and with her incredible drive and determination, who can doubt that she will rock the world off the soccer field as well.

How Will You Rock the World?

"My sister had eye cancer and now has a fake eye. I know how hard it is for her, so I will become an ophthalmologist and find a cure for eye cancer."

Tierney Brennecke, age 11

"I would like to be a role model for girls who have sports dreams. So, I will rock the world by becoming a well-known, inspiring soccer player."

Sarah Potter, age 12

"I will rock the world by being the best Women's U.S. soccer player, just like Mia Hamm."

Hannah Schiff, age 7

Lauryn Hill

1975– ◼ *Singer/Songwriter/Producer* ◼ *United States*

I don't feel like my money or my success defines me. I've always been very happy just bein' me.
— Lauryn Hill

She couldn't wait for the movie to start. The theater went dark, the projector lit up, and Lauryn watched Little Orphan Annie dancing and singing across the huge screen. Hundreds of eyes were on this girl. Hundreds of people applauded for her when the movie was over. At school, all her friends were talking about this girl. That's what Lauryn wanted, too; she wanted to dance and sing for people. She wanted people to clap for her, too. The only difference between her and this girl was that she was black and the little girl on the screen was white.

"Mommy, could there ever be a black Annie?"

Lauryn's mother laughed and rolled her eyes, "That'll be the day!" But she didn't say no. She knew by now that no matter what she told her seven-year-old daughter, Lauryn would make up her own mind anyway. If Lauryn wanted to be the first black Annie, she certainly couldn't talk her out of it.

Lauryn has probably given up on starring in *Annie*, but she hasn't stopped stretching her mind and the minds of those around her as to what is possible for a black girl to do. Whether she was getting straight As in high school while starring in a soap opera *and* singing in a hip-hop band, or writing feminist rap songs and producing her own hit album in a male-dominated industry, Lauryn always seemed to be asking, "And why *can't* I do that?"

The Queen of Hip-Hop was born in South Orange, New Jersey. Her father, a computer analyst, and her mother, a high school English teacher, raised Lauryn in a happy, loving, supportive home. It was clear from the beginning she was a performer. Lauryn remembers her big childhood dreams, "When I was a very little girl, I wanted to be a superstar-slash-lawyer-slash-doctor." She always loved music. She began singing with her church choir and in gospel groups as a young girl, formed her first singing group before she was ten, and was writing her own song lyrics in middle school.

Although Lauryn grew up in a middle-class neighborhood, from her bedroom window she could see the projects where her poorer friends lived. She was always aware of the problems they and other African-Americans struggled with.

She was thirteen when she first began performing in public. She sang at the Apollo Theatre in Harlem, in a live show (an early version of *Star Search*) that was televised nationally. The show was brutal; if the crowd didn't like you, they booed until you left the stage in shame. Not only did the live audience witness your humiliation, but millions of TV viewers did, too. Superstars like Ella Fitzgerald, James Brown, and the Jackson Five had survived this ordeal and gone on to fame. Lauryn wanted her chance. When she got on stage to sing, she didn't stand close enough to the microphone. The audience couldn't hear her. Instead of panicking when the boos started, Lauryn grabbed the mike and sang her heart out. In the end, she won over the crowd, and they screamed for more.

That same year, her cousin Prakazrel "Pras" Michel, the son of Haitian immigrants, tapped Lauryn to sing in his new hip-hop band, Time. Later Pras added another cousin to the band, Wyclef "Clef" Jean, a recent arrival from impoverished Haiti. Lauryn dubbed herself "Haitian by association" and the band started playing New York and New Jersey nightclubs, hoping to be discovered by a record company.

But primary in Lauryn's mind was school. She may not have been a superstar of the radio yet, but she was a superstar of Columbia High. She got almost perfect grades, played on the basketball team, was captain of the cheerleading squad, and was voted class president. She even started a gospel choir and a breakfast program for kids at her school who couldn't afford their own. And she planned to go to college when she graduated.

But her pursuit of fame was the extracurricular activity she worked hardest at. Freshman year, she landed a role in an off-Broadway hip-hop musical, *Club 12*; sophomore year, she snagged a part in the soap opera *As the World Turns*. Her dreams were coming true, but she was almost too busy to enjoy herself. Lauryn went to high school in New Jersey in the mornings, to tape the soap opera in New York City in the afternoons, and to gigs with Time in the evenings. "I remember doing my homework in the bathroom stalls of hip-hop clubs," Lauryn recalled of her busy teen years.

At the start of her senior year, the band got its big break. A scout for Ruffhouse Records caught one of their shows and offered them a recording contract. As they began working on their first album, *Blunted on Reality*, the band decided it was time to change their name to reflect their heritage and beliefs. They renamed themselves The Fugees, short for refugees. The name expressed pride in their Haitian backgrounds, as well their social views, "As people of African descent," Pras explained, "we are all refugees. Everyone came to this country on a boat at one time or another." They finished the album by Lauryn's graduation.

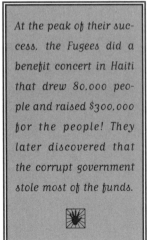

At the peak of their success, the Fugees did a benefit concert in Haiti that drew 80,000 people and raised $300,000 for the people! They later discovered that the corrupt government stole most of the funds.

With the album complete, Lauryn turned her focus back to academics. She had applied to and been accepted by several Ivy League colleges. She chose Columbia University because its New York City campus was closest to her family, the band, and other show biz opportunities. While starting college and waiting for the release of *Blunted on Reality*, Lauryn continued drama auditions. She won a nationwide talent search for the movie *Sister Act II* with Whoopi Goldberg, and played an inner-city, gospel-singing teen. She finally got to see herself singing and dancing up on the big screen—her childhood fantasy. The movie got panned, but critics loved Lauryn. Roger Ebert of the *Chicago Sun-Times* praised the "big, joyful musical voice and luminous smile" of this unknown talent.

But Lauryn wouldn't remain unknown for long. The Fugees were becoming more and more popular and began touring to promote their album. Lauryn had a tough choice to make; she couldn't give 100% to college *and* to her career. With some fear in her heart, she quit Columbia and went for her music dreams. With Lauryn's full attention on music, the Fugees began work on a second album. This time, instead of just singing, Lauren wrote, arranged, and produced many of the songs

The Ms. Foundation named Lauryn one of the Top 10 Role Models for 1999.

as well. Female record producers were rare, indeed, but with her show biz experience, Lauryn felt ready for the job. By the end of 1995, *The Score* was ready for release. Lauryn was twenty years old.

The Score shot up the charts, racking up sales of nearly 18 million CDs. Almost overnight, the Fugees became the biggest-selling rap group in history. They also won over the critics. *Entertainment Weekly* praised their "acrobatic lyrical technique and restless intelligence," while *Time* magazine called the Fugees a band that "crossed cultural and musical boundaries to create a sound that is bold and fresh." They won two Grammy Awards, Best Rap Album and Best R&B Performance, for Lauryn's wildly popular hip-hop cover of Roberta Flack's "Killing Me Softly." Lauryn, Pras, and Clef were bona fide stars.

From the very beginning of the Fugees, Lauryn got most of the attention because of her incredible voice and stunning looks. Many people advised her to drop the band and go solo, and reporters wrote very public (and, to Lauryn, embarrassing) articles about how Lauryn was carrying the Fugees. But Pras and Clef were like brothers to Lauryn; she ignored the advice. She went so far as to reject any solo projects that came her way and even seemed to downplay her role in the band, highlighting the contributions of her bandmates instead.

But Lauryn's humility backfired. Clef and Pras felt no guilt taking on solo projects without her, and when they were successful, the media turned on Lauryn, claiming she was just the voice and the guys were the real geniuses of the band. "It's as though men can write 'serious compositions' but women just sing 'cute little ditties,'" she griped. When her bandmates didn't defend her, Lauryn grew depressed, and in the midst of her greatest success, she began doubting her abilities to write and compose music.

Lauryn experienced a strange catalyst, however. Although she had always had a troubled love life, she finally met and fell in love with a man who shared her values. Rohan Marley, son of reggae legend Bob Marley, was not intimidated by Lauryn's talent and success, was good to her, and loved her just as much as she loved him. When Lauryn accidentally got pregnant, she was torn about what to do. Almost everyone told her that having a baby at that moment would be the worst mistake of her life; it would ruin her career. But Lauryn disagreed. She loved the child's father and planned to spend her life with him. She loved kids, too, and she could easily afford to raise a family on her own if she had to. She decided to have her child.

One of the most popular songs on The Miseducation of Lauryn Hill, "Going to Zion," was inspired by the birth of her son, Zion.

Being pregnant transformed Lauryn. "When some women are pregnant, their hair and nails grow," she said, "My mind and ability to create expanded." She poured all her feelings into her songs—her joy in being pregnant and being in love, her anger and feelings of betrayal, her creative insecurities and triumphs. "Every time I got hurt," she said, "every time I was disappointed, every time I learned, I just wrote a song." Although many people in the business thought she should just do another "Killing Me Softly," Lauryn wrote songs that were very different and all her own.

She decided to create her own album, finally going solo. She not only wrote and sang all the songs for it, she also produced it entirely on her own. Lauryn explains her move into what's considered "male territory":

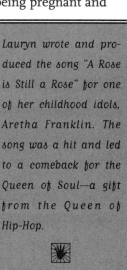

Lauryn wrote and produced the song "A Rose is Still a Rose" for one of her childhood idols, Aretha Franklin. The song was a hit and led to a comeback for the Queen of Soul—a gift from the Queen of Hip-Hop.

Music is so important to me and how I come across is so important. I'm a perfectionist. If I have to do it a hundred times, I'll do it a hundred times![24]

Her perfectionism paid off. When *The Miseducation of Lauryn Hill* was released in 1998, it hit the charts with supreme force. Lauryn's honest, uplifting, spiritual and deeply personal album chronicled her journey from naïve youth to musical maverick. It debuted at number one and sold 420,000 copies in the first week, a new record for female singers. It eventually went triple-platinum.

The critics, too, were in heaven. *Spin* magazine praised the album's "almost unnerving perfection," and *Entertainment Weekly* christened it "Album of the Year" and "one of the most forceful statements ever by a woman in pop." Lauryn was further honored with a record *ten* Grammy nominations in 1999 (the most ever for a woman). She won five (again, a record for women): Best R&B Album, Best R&B Song, Best Female R&B Vocal Performance, Best New Artist, and Best Album of the Year.

In spite of her huge achievements, Lauryn always sees her music as a platform for getting her message to the people and creating social change. She founded and chairs the Refugee Project, a non-profit organization dedicated to changing the lives of at-risk, inner-city kids who need a boost. Lauryn believes that any person who has few options for escaping a dangerous society is a refugee. Her vision is to inspire troubled kids to triumph over obstacles in their path, through programs that encourage eleven "core values": courage, peace, discipline, faith, strength, determination, wisdom, excellence, service, knowledge, and love. She also works to get businesses involved, and to provide kids with entrepreneurial and professional opportunities.

One of Lauryn's first efforts with the Refugee Project was to organize a free concert in Harlem encouraging voter registration in the African-American community. People thought she was crazy. But "Hoodshock," as it was dubbed, boasted a roster of stars like the Wu-Tang Clan, Sean "Puffy" Combs, and the Notorious B.I.G., and drew a crowd of 10,000 peaceful rap fans.

Throughout her life, Lauryn has faced all the stereotypes—women aren't good at business, can't write intelligent music, can't produce albums; rap singers can't have a hit unless they sing about guns, drugs, sex, and money. Lauryn has broken every rule. As a girl, she proved that she could become a star and still get a good education, and as an adult, she shocked the music world by writing, arranging, and producing her own hit album. As the *San*

Francisco Examiner put it, Lauryn's success, ". . . reveals her deep intellect and creativity, as well as her business sense." No one can say Lauryn Hill is just a pretty face.

> *And every time I try to be*
> *What someone has thought of me*
> *So caught up, I wasn't able to achieve*
> *But deep in my heart the answer it was in me*
> *And I made up my mind to find my own destiny*
> — lyrics from "The Miseducation of Lauryn Hill"

How Will You Rock the World?

"I'm happiest when I'm singing. I want to become a role model who can help kids grow up strong, healthy and drug-free. I've joined a chorus to practice and  am trying to record my songs to send to record companies. Remember the name—Jennifer Frost—I might hit it big someday!"

Jennifer Frost, age 12

"I would rock the world by helping kids who have AIDS. I'll set up a camp for them, since most camps don't allow  these kids in because of their disease. These kids are normal people who have a disease that is hard to catch."

Michelle Agee, age 12

Girls Who Are Rocking the World Right Now!

Kory Johnson

1980— ❋ *ENVIRONMENTAL ACTIVIST* ❋ *UNITED STATES*

Young people everywhere are entitled to environmental justice, no matter what their color or socioeconomic status. — Kory Johnson

When Kory was nine, her older sister died of heart problems. She did some investigating and discovered that many other people in her inner-city neighborhood were dying; in fact, the area was a "cancer cluster" (a place where the number of people getting cancer is much higher than average). Kory figured out that her sister probably died because her mother unknowingly drank contaminated well water while pregnant.

Determined to take action, Kory formed Children for a Safe Environment (CSE), a group that encourages young people, especially those living in poor neighborhoods, to speak out against environmental health hazards. Unethical companies target these areas to dump industrial waste and other toxic materials. They figure that poor people don't have the time, money, or knowledge to fight back. Kory and CSE are showing them just how wrong they are.

In 1991, CSE battled the state of Arizona, which planned to dump all the state's hazardous waste into a poor neighborhood. CSE organized protests and got the media's attention. And it won! The governor of Arizona canceled the plans for the dump site. Kory, who is Native American and Mexican American herself, also worked with a group of Native Americans in California to fight a radioactive waste dump planned for their area.

When she started CSE, Kory's teachers warned her that her "radical" activism would hurt her chances of getting into college. Kory, however, had no problems getting into Arizona State University. Winning the prestigious Goldman Environmental Prize in 1998 for a heroic contribution to environmentalism probably didn't hurt. Part of Kory's prize was a $125,000 scholarship! The Ms. Foundation also named her one of the Top 10 Role Models for 1999. Aside from winning awards and going to school, Kory now spends her time traveling America and teaching people about the hazards of industrial pollution and how to stand up for their rights.

Jennifer Fletcher

1982– ✿ *Concert Promoter* ✿ *United States*

People [don't] realize how much the arts mean to students . . .
for many people it is their only chance to express themselves.

— Jennifer Fletcher

The voters in Jennifer's hometown of Portland, Oregon, had cut the city's public school budget. Many schools had to get rid of art, music, dance, and drama classes, so that only kids who could afford private lessons could participate in the arts. When Jennifer was a high school sophomore, her drama teacher told the class that if they wanted to stage the musical *Oliver!*, they'd have to help pay for it out of their own pockets. She was appalled.

Jennifer decided to stage a benefit concert to raise money that could be used to bring arts classes back to the public schools. Most people scoffed when she told them she planned to get Jackson Browne, one of her favorite singers, to play at the concert and that she would raise at least $50,000.

Jackson Browne gets tons of requests to play benefit concerts. Why would hers be any different? But when he read Jennifer's eloquent letter, he was blown away. He said "Yes!"

The show sold out in four days. Jennifer handled all the logistics of staging the huge event like a pro, and on October 29, 1998, Jackson Browne played in a large Portland concert hall. Jennifer even got the hall to discount its normal fee. To distribute the benefit's proceeds (close to $100,000) Jennifer created ARTS ALIVE!, a nonprofit organization. Schools apply for money for arts projects, and Jennifer and other students decide exactly where the money goes. "The students know what is most needed," she explained. No adults are involved in the decision-making.

In 1999, Jennifer won the *Seventeen* magazine Volunteerism Award, which earned her a $10,000 college scholarship, $10,000 for ARTS ALIVE!, and dinner with First Lady Hillary Clinton. At the award ceremony, Jennifer was praised as "a young woman of extraordinary vision and passion for making things right." But Jennifer doesn't want to organize concerts for a living; she hopes to go to Stanford and become a horticultural scientist!

Nicole McLaren

1985– ✤ Web Delegate ✤ Jamaica

A lot of young people don't feel they can influence the decisions that affect them. We know that's not true, and we're going to change it. — Nicole McLaren

When Nicole left her home in Jamaica for Boston, Massachusetts, to attend the 1998 Junior Summit at the Massachusetts Institute of Technology (MIT), she had no idea she'd return home and create a new nation. But that's just what she did. Nicole had been concerned about kids' lack of connection to world events and their feelings of helplessness in the face of global problems. She wanted to create a "nation" for young people, a place where they could meet and discuss international issues, debate politics, and work on solving some of the world's biggest problems.

To Nicole, the Internet was the perfect stomping ground for a global youth movement. In cyberspace there are no borders, no skin colors, no religious differences. So she created Nation 1 (*www.nation1.com*). "Nation 1 breaks down all of these [differences] and encourages cross-cultural interaction," Nicole explains, "When we're on the Internet, we're just one nation." Nation 1 even takes care of language differences so visitors to the site can communicate with practically anyone in the world.

Nicole has even bigger plans for Nation 1. Soon the site will show kids how to get involved with regional and global projects that interest them, find people with money to help fund their ideas, and hear the latest international news from the kids who are there. By bringing global youth together, Nation 1 will join their voices, concerns, and actions into a powerful force in the world.

Corporations like Swatch, Compaq, Apple, Motorola and UNESCO have already recognized the wisdom of Nicole's idea. They are partnering with Nation 1 to help it achieve its goals. Nicole's current project is recruiting four hundred youth representatives to the next United Nations assembly. She wants the group to talk to world leaders about issues that are important to young people, such as education and kids in the military. When asked about what kids can do, Nicole responds, "I think the sky's the limit."

Alexandra Nechita

1985– ⊕ PAINTER ⊕ ROMANIA/UNITED STATES

I like to know that people are looking at my paintings and are
trying to find the story behind them. It is different than just looking—
they are thinking as well. — Alexandra Nechita

Alexandra's parents were worried. Their four-year-old didn't play with dolls like her friends. All she wanted to do was draw. They took away her coloring books, hoping she'd find other ways to have fun. But Alexandra couldn't stop. She just started drawing on any scrap of paper she could find. Her parents gave up and gave her crayons back.

At school all her friends drew regular people, square houses, and brown dogs. But Alexandra had a difficult time drawing realistically, saying, "I can't express myself . . . It's not my natural way." Instead, she drew green heads with four eyes and blue noses under their chins. Her stuff did not look normal at all. But by the time she turned nine, she was showing her paintings in art galleries and libraries and was attracting huge crowds. People compared her to Picasso and Matisse, but her style is all her own. Her favorite themes—peace, family, nature, and happiness—shine through in every canvas.

By age ten, she was one of the hottest-selling artists in America. Her work is on display in twenty museums and has sold to over a thousand private collectors—including stars like Whoopi Goldberg and Oprah Winfrey! At the age of eight, Alexandra sold her first painting for $50, but now they sell for between $15,000 to $125,000! She has already earned nearly $3 million!

And she's not just famous in America; she's had exhibits in Paris, Geneva, Singapore, and Tokyo as well. She doesn't let the money, the awards, or the television interviews go to her head. "I'm just a normal child," she says, "I go to school, I come back, I start painting." Lately, she has worked with UNICEF to raise money for children, and has created art for the Grammy Awards. Recently, the Van Gogh Institute awarded her the Gold Key Honor and the United Nations even made her an Ambassador of Peace and Goodwill! Most artists' works develop and change over their careers. It will be fascinating to see how Alexandra, already famous at fifteen, will evolve as she gets older.

Charlotte Church

1986– ✎ SINGER ✎ WALES

*Charlotte is a phenomenon. She is gifted beyond her years, and
her voice has a clarity and quality that will surprise and captivate
audiences the world over.*

— Thomas Mottola, Chairman, Sony Music Entertainment

Charlotte was proud of her grades: 92 in music, 87 in French, and 87 in history. These numbers tell the story of a hardworking student, one whose tutor makes her work three hours a day on her lessons. What they don't tell is that, at that same time Charlotte was studying French verbs, she was on her way to becoming one of the most successful recording artists of today.

In the year that 12-year-old Charlotte earned those good grades, she earned a few other good numbers—like two million CDs sold! Her first CD, *Voice of An Angel*, made it into the top five in the United Kingdom. In that year, she also sang for Prince Charles's fiftieth birthday, for the Pope at Christmas, and, on her first visit to America, for President Clinton.

Charlotte had a very, very good year. But her life as a singer started nine years earlier, when she was three. She and her family were vacationing in Wales when she and her sister belted out the theme from *Ghostbusters* to a delighted crowd. At the age of eight, she answered a television show's request for talented kids to enter a contest. When she called and said she could sing, the voice on the end of the line said, "Prove it!" She did—big time! She ended up appearing on that show and others. These appearances led to a recording contract with Sony. Since then she's released her second CD, *Charlotte Church*.

Where does a wildly successful singer (with good grades) go from here? Charlotte says she plans to train her voice further in the classical way (opera). Her career ambition is to sing at the world's most famous opera house, La Scala, in Milan, Italy, in one of the world's most haunting operas, *Madame Butterfly*.

Notes

1. Chi D. Nguyen. "Trung Trac & Trung Nhi." www.viettouch.com/trung_sisters_main.html (January 10, 2000).

2. Elisabeth Vigée-Le Brun, trans. Siân Evans. *The Memoirs of Elisabeth Vigée-Le Brun* (Indianapolis: Indiana University Press, 1989), 11.

3. Vigée-Le Brun, 32.

4. Vigée-Le Brun, 2.

5. Meriwether Lewis. *The Journals of the Lewis and Clark Expedition*, vol. 5, ed. Gary E. Moulton (Lincoln, Nebraska: University of Nebraska Press, 1988), 109.

6. Susanna Reich. *Clara Schumann: Piano Virtuoso* (New York: Clarion Books, 1999), 17.

7. Reich, 30.

8. M.W. Taylor. *Harriet Tubman: Antislavery Activist* (New York and Philadelphia: Chelsea House, 1991), 37.

9. Anne Macdonald. *Feminine Ingenuity: Women and Invention in America* (New York: Ballantine, 1992), 51.

10. A. H. Franks. *Pavlova: A Biography* (New York: Da Capo Press, 1956), 15-16.

11. Russell Freedman. *Eleanor Roosevelt: Life of Discovery* (New York: Clarion Books, 1993), 23.

12. Rachel Toor. *Eleanor Roosevelt: Diplomat and Humanitarian* (New York: Chelsea House, 1989), 65.

13. Eileen Whitfield. *Pickford: The Woman Who Made Hollywood* (Lexington, Kentucky: University Press of Kentucky, 1997), 19.

14. James Farmer. *Eleanor Roosevelt* (PBS, Portland, Oregon, 1999).

15. Bruce Myles. *Night Witches: The Untold Story of Soviet Women in Combat* (Novato, California: Presidio, 1981), 6.

16. Harold Stockton, Dariusz Tyminski, and Christer Bergström. "Marina Raskova and Soviet Female Pilots." www.elknet.pl/acestory/raskov/raskov.htm (January 4, 2000).

17. Stockton.

18. Myles, 145.

19. George Mair. *Oprah Winfrey: The Real Story* (New York: Carol Publishing, 1994), 8.

20. Janet Lowe. *Oprah Winfrey Speaks* (New York: John Wiley & Sons, 1998), 10.

21. Mair, 31.

22. Bob Italia. *Maya Lin: Honoring Our Forgotten Heroes* (Minneapolis: Abdo & Daughters, 1993), 7-9.

23. Peter Potterfield. "Lynn Hill: Climbing Through the Glass Ceiling." www.mountainzone.com/climbing/99/interviews/hill (February 16, 2000).

24. "The Miseducation of Lauryn Hill." www.lauryn-hill.com/history.html (January 4, 2000).

How Will You Rock the World?

PLEASE DO NOT WRITE IN THIS BOOK! Photocopy this page and fill out your information in the spaces provided. Handwritten is fine. Mail your completed page to:

More Girls Who Rocked the World
Beyond Words Publishing, Inc.
20827 N.W. Cornell Road, Suite 500
Hillsboro, Oregon 97124-9808

Name _____ **Age** _____

Address _____

City _____ **State** _____ **Zip Code** _____

Phone Number (_____)_____ (to call you if you win. Beyond Words Publishing will not call you for any other reason.)

Write your dreams here:

Put your photo here:

You could be included in the next book.

Glossary

Amazons: tall, strong, usually masculine women who, according to legend, were female warriors.

bondage: the state of being captive, bound, or unwillingly under the control of some powerful, and often harsh, authority; slavery.

cabaret: a place that serves food and drink, especially liquor, and provides entertainment that usually includes singing and dancing.

chauvinism: behavior that displays an attitude of superiority over the opposite sex.

consort: an associate or partner, usually in some kind of official business.

debutante: a young woman, usually upper-class, who makes a formal "first" appearance to enter society.

hydrometry: a study of the gravity and strength of liquids.

"Jim Crow" laws: the legal enforcement of segregation between different races, particularly blacks and whites, that outlawed interracial marriages and required separate public facilities, including schools, transportation, and medical care.

kibbutz: a farm or settlement in Israel where residents live and work together as a small, cooperative community.

longhouse: a long building in which members of certain tribes of Native Americans shared living space.

lynching: executing a supposed criminal by the action of a mob, usually by hanging, without a lawful trial and conviction.

machismo: an overblown sense of male power, strength, and pride.

metaphysics: the branch of philosophy that deals with the science of being or existing and with the relationships between all forms of existence throughout the cosmos.

mill: a type of factory equipped with machinery for grinding, weaving, or performing other kinds of repetitive, mechanical actions.

molested: disturbed or persecuted in a hostile way, usually resulting in physical injury and, often, forced sexual contact.

nickelodeon: the first kind of movie theater for which a ticket cost a nickel.

patent: (n) an official document that guarantees the exclusive right to make, use, or sell a particular invention.

patriarchal: related to a society, group, or family controlled by a father or father figure.

tar paper: heavy tar-coated paper often used in the construction of buildings.

thwart: to effectively stop, oppose, or defeat the actions or plans of another.

Zionists: people who support an international movement to establish a Jewish national homeland in Israel.

More Books to Read

100 Most Important Women of the 20th Century. Kevin Markey, et al (Meredith Books)

All-American Girls: The U.S. Women's National Soccer Team. Marla Miller (Econo-Clad Books)

Chanel: Her Style and Her Life. Janet Wallach (Doubleday)

Charlotte Brontë. The British Library Writers' Lives (series). Jane Sellars (Oxford University Press)

Clara Schumann: Piano Virtuoso. Susanna Reich (Clarion Books)

Eleanor Roosevelt: A Life of Discovery. Russell Freedman (Econo-Clad Books)

Florence Nightingale: War Nurse. Anne Colver (Chelsea House)

Naya Nuki: Shoshoni Girl Who Ran. Kenneth Thomasma (Grandview)

On the Field with . . . Mia Hamm. Matt Christopher (Little Brown & Co.)

Our Golda: The Story of Golda Meir. David Adler (Econo-Clad Books)

The Story of Harriet Tubman: Conductor of the Underground Railroad. Famous Lives (series). Kate McMullan (Gareth Stevens)

Videos

The American Experience: Eleanor Roosevelt. (PBS Home Video)

A Century of Women. (Turner Home Entertainment)

The Famous Authors Series: The Brontë Sisters. (White Star Video)

The Hidden Army: Women in World War II. (Goldhil Home Media International)

Maya Lin: A Strong Clear Vision. (Tapeworm Video)

Underground Railroad. (A & E Home Video)

Web Sites

Florence Nightingale Museum. (www.florence-nightingale.co.uk)

Mary Louise Elisabeth Vigee-Lebrun. (www.printmasterinc.com/colors/lebrun.html)

My Hero: Anyone Can Be a Hero. (www.myhero.com/home.asp)

Sonja Henie Snapshot. (www.zianet.com/jjohnson/sonja/index.htm)

Vietnamese National Heroines: Trung Sisters. (www.boatpeople.com/heroes_heroines/trung_sister.html)

To find additional Web sites, use a reliable search engine with one or more of the following keywords: *actresses, artists, athletes, authors, ballet, climbing, girls, heroines, history, musicians, nursing, Olympics, politics, singers, women.* (You can also search by entering any individual name.)

Index